For my wife Gracia Fay,
    who taught me to love his appearing.

Contents

1
FROM JAMES BOND TO JESUS: AMERICAN POPULAR CULTURE IN THE SIXTIES 1

The Metamorphoses of Popular Culture, 1   Psychedelic Culture and Jesus Culture, 11

2
EVANGELICALISM IN AMERICA 24

Religion on American Soil, 24   The Official Temple and the Short Path, 27   Evangelical Teaching and Practice, 30   Evangelicalism and Society, 35   The Story of American Evangelicalism, 38   Pentecostalism, 44

3
THE JESUS EXPERIENCE 51

The Jesus Movement as Religious Experience, 51   The Central Religious Motif of the Jesus Movement, 54   The Jesus Movement and the Forms of Religious Expression, 57   The

Story of the Movement, 59   Symbols and Music of the Movement, 63   The Movement and the Evangelical Alternative World, 70

4
THE TRANSCENDENCE OF TIME   72

Time and Religion, 72   Calvary Chapel, 73   Mansion Messiah, 76   The Church in Los Angeles, 78   Sharing the Sufferings of God's People, 82   The Christian Foundation, 83   Responses to Time, 85

5
RESPONSES TO HISTORY   86

History and Apocalyptic Time, 86   The Apocalyptic Vision, 88   Hal Lindsey and Jesus Movement Apocalyptic, 89   Bethel Tabernacle, 93   Arthur Blessitt, 95

6
COMMUNES AND THE CHILDREN OF GOD   97

Communes and Apocalyptic Sects, 97   The Children of God, 101   The Story of the Children, 106

7
ON THE CAMPUS   112

The Inter-Varsity Christian Fellowship, 113   Campus Crusade for Christ, 114   The Christian World Liberation Front, 117   Evangelicalism, Campus Groups, and the Jesus Movement, 119

8
OTHER ALTERNATIVES   121

The Metropolitan Community Church, 122   Catholic Pentecostalism, 125   The Mythopoeic Society, 128   The Process, 130

9
**THE MOVEMENT AND CHRISTIANITY
IN THE TWENTY-FIRST CENTURY 132**

NOTES 142

BIBLIOGRAPHY 145

INDEX 147

Introduction

*I*N THE EARLY YEARS of the 1970s the Jesus movement was one of the most talked about of American religious phenomena. Young people in considerable numbers were rejecting both conventional Christianity and "counter culture" religions to take up with evangelical Christianity. Incense and soft chants to Krishna or Buddha gave place to the sawdust and joyous hallelujahs of frontier-type camp meetings.

To many observers the new Christianity appeared as a sudden and unexpected shock. In the late sixties the spiritual future seemed to lie almost wholly either with political activism in the churches or with the many new groups offering expansion of consciousness: meditation movements, chanting cults, Scientology, magic, and Witchcraft. I have described a number of these groups in a previous book, *Religious and Spiritual Groups in Modern America.*

One afternoon at about the time I was finishing that book, I walked down Hollywood Boulevard. This fabled street, its sidewalks set with the names of movie stars, has long been a haven for current emergent, counter, or stillborn cultural variants. I passed occult bookstores, headshops, and purveyors of the herbs and oils of Witchcraft. Nearby was an apartment where I had once visited a conference of ceremonial magicians and Satanists; not far away was a hall where I had seen disciples of Gurdijieffian techniques endeavoring to chant and exercise themselves into the Fourth State of Consciousness. On this street the colorful saffron-robed devotees of Krishna had often danced and sung.

Today, though, there was something new. A pair of young men with long hair and a fixed, clear gaze, wearing levis and denim jackets, patrolled a corner near Hollywood and Vine. They were handing every passerby a slip of paper exhorting him to repent and accept Christ, for Christ is coming soon. The Jesus movement had come.

The movement's visibility increased at an exponential rate. Quickly, not only slips of paper but tracts and throwaway Christian newspapers blanketed the Boulevard. People wore crosses, some said as protection against the Satanists still lurking in the city. I heard of arguments on street corners between rival proclaimers of salvation as to whether Krishna or Jesus was better. But soon, aided by the dominant culture, Jesus had his thousands to Krishna's hundreds—at least in the U.S.A.

Then there was such a rush of magazines, newspapers, and TV specials featuring the Jesus "boom" that it could not be avoided. As usual the media doubtless did as much to create as to describe the phenomenon. Nationwide churches and evangelical organizations leaped with alacrity to make the movement validate what they had always said, and at the same time to shore up their position by adopting its rhetoric and style. They employed the songs and signs and art of the movement to revitalize their own work with youth, and in this manner the movement or its echoes reached millions who had not heard the "underground" word. Next came books about the movement.[1]

This book, *One Way,* attempts to deal with the Jesus movement in a new way. I have wanted to look at it first within the context of American culture, and secondly in terms of parallels brought in from the history of religion in many times and places. We will see how the Jesus movement compares with frontier revivalism, Tibetan religion, and many other things.

In the course of these observations, I hope to provide insights which will aid the reader in understanding—from within—what the Jesus movement is doing in the lives of its adherents, and in the culture of America. Even more important, I hope I have done something to illustrate the nature of evangelicalism, popular culture, and the present religious situation in America.

I am very grateful to all of those within the movement, or close to it, with whom I have talked. They have all been unfailingly kind and helpful. I am particularly appreciative of the historical information and interpretative insights given by the Rev. Donald M. Williams of the Hollywood Presbyterian Church. While probably none of my informants would agree with all the opinions and viewpoints expressed in this book, and are not responsible for them, their help has made it possible and I value them deeply as Christians and as friends.

1

From James Bond to Jesus: American Popular Culture in the Sixties

THE METAMORPHOSES OF POPULAR CULTURE

THERE IS A GAME called "Fool the Prophets." Though it is a diversion of ridiculous simplicity, it is also a great delight. What it consists of is this: The ordinary people listen very attentively while the wise pundits and prophets dilate at length on what the future will bring. They consider the graphs and tables and the analyses and projections of trends unveiled by the learned. The ordinary people thank the wise ones, doubtlessly rewarding them handsomely. Then they go and do something else.

"Fool the Prophets" has been played on a sweeping scale in American popular and political culture in the sixties and seventies. Never have predictions and projections been more plentiful and precise. Never have the people who make popular culture taken more apparent delight in confounding the prognostications by finding something else to do.

The "playing field" for the game of pop culture has been called "accessible fantasy" by Margot Hentoff. It is a pleasure garden whose groves resound with the sort of songs one hears on the car radio, whose tree trunks are plastered with the titles of best-selling books, whose grottos flicker with the favorite movies and TV shows, interspersed with familiar advertising motifs and political images of the day.

The basic point of pop culture is that it is a culture of *images* rather than of a literary heritage and an historical consciousness. Pop culture does not consider desirable goals or states of consciousness possible only at the end of long spans of bookish study, or practice of spiritual techniques, much less at the end of aeons of historical process or cosmic evolution. A pop culture man is too busy working at a job, or getting a diploma, or marrying and raising a family. While of course he reads, a cultural world really grounded on what he gets out of books or on techniques for which only a few have leisure is not for him. His image-filled world is closer to that of folk religion, or to those vast ages of man before the invention of writing—the world of the mask, the temple image, and the ecstatic dance around the fire. Pop culture shares folk religion's profundity, immediacy of experience, and limitations. In this world most of us live most of the time.

Because it lacks history's vision of the present as only a fragment of a very long process, the goals of pop culture must be always accessible, available here and now as present images. In unlettered archaic religion, the numinous power and presence of the gods had to be immediately present in the temple festivals. In pop culture, too, the promise and the fulfillment must be telescoped to where only an easy and minimal time span separates them. You no sooner think of the ideal glamour girl, for example, than you see her on TV or in the movies. There is an idea of deferred reward—work now to get something you want later—but it involves manageable dimensions of time: save now for a new house, wait to travel until you are older, work during the week to have a good time on the weekend.

These sorts of goals, however, do not always satisfy humankind's deep unspoken longings. The "glamour girl" (even if you marry her) is not always the Eternal Feminine; the movie hero is not really the Eternal Hero, able to conquer even the fear of death. So pop culture is always changing and searching. But when it turns from one image to another, from one glamour girl or hero to the next, it does not attain historical awareness (though individuals may). It does not conclude, "Because we have found these images to be partial, we can now deduce that all images are partial, conditioned by the time and place which brought them forth." Rather it moves by sudden, apocalyptic[2] strokes, often creating a radical reversal of present motifs. Apocalyptic events are by definition unpredictable, at least by ordinary means. Since pop culture knows change, but does not comprehend or really accept slow historical time, it thinks of change only as sudden and unexpected, like the changing of a television channel or the unexpected vision of the ideal beloved "across a crowded room." The expectation fulfills itself; individuals affected by it will suddenly change the course of their lives. The entire complex of symbols of a pop culture will suddenly radically reverse its whole tone. When dress styles and songs and books abruptly change their mood, it is as though a shaman or prophet had persuasively brought the image of a new god to some archaic tribe. The new in each case is absolute for its time, for the gods have no past or future.

The apocalyptic motif keeps pop culture enlivened by a deep, secret air of mystery in its hidden core. "Ah, Sweet Mystery of Life" could be its theme song. The apocalyptic mystery keeps the game of "Fool the Prophets" forever playable. It also gives pop culture the added range which helps it reflect—often better than intellectual culture—the subtle rhythms and the unexpectedness of the universe itself.

In pop culture nothing is more permanent than change. From a life of problem solving and celebrating the "secular city" in the fifties and early sixties, we moved in the mid-sixties to one of mystical expansion of consciousness, and then later to an atmosphere fomenting revolutionary change in the structures of society. Now, suddenly, posters and bumper stickers appear with pictures of Jesus Christ and messages like One Way and Read the Bible. Rock groups on the radio and in coffeehouses with names like Kentucky Faith and The Salt Company belt out evangelical hymns old and new. Each stage offers its own reward.

In the early sixties, we moved out of the Eisenhower years of suburban apotheosis and the organization man to the accompaniment of winsome folk songs. We read novels about the various "corridors of power" convoluted by a complex civilization itself amazed at the incredible knowledge, skill, and sense of balance its perpetuation required. These corridors ran through networks of government offices, academia, the military, business, and espionage, surfacing in English country houses and American suburban bedrooms. The novels buzzed with the low chatter of elegant cocktail parties, and the hushed rattle of papers being stuffed into briefcases. We liked to imagine, at least, that we lived in the world created by C.P. Snow, James Cozzens, and Ian Fleming. Only a James Bond could handle this world with cool finesse and breezy aplomb. But more likely we were part of the world of the hero in John Updike's novel *Rabbit, Run,* who listened to all the pop songs on the car radio as he left his wife and finally turned toward the frothy pop religion of the Rev. Mr. Eccles.

I was an undergraduate and graduate student off and on during those years. I can remember hayrides sponsored by church groups, dress and dating ceremony and proms probably more similar to usages of the czarist court than the happenings of the psychedelic era. Students usually went to Europe during the summers if they went anywhere, and no one thought much about India.

But American global policy sometimes dictated other travel plans. I spent 1961, a year I have since regarded as the zenith of the *pax americana,* on Okinawa. My principal memory of that year seems to be almost assimilated with a mental image of Kipling's India. I see myself sitting on the veranda of the officer's club, set strikingly on the highest ground around the base, surveying through the humid air the barracks of the sweaty green-clad Marines. Beyond them lay the base gates, neatly terraced rice fields, quaint thatched roof villages, and finally the coral tinted sea with its still fishing boats. The older officers talked of the heroic days of battle and glory in Tarawa and Saipan and Korea, of the triumphant confusion of the Occupation in Japan, and of other American military valhallas in Tientsin and Sasebo. Parties in military clubs frequently had the same tinselly Japanese motif decorations—the pop culture of an affable and gregarious military society, fascinated by its world of arms and prestige, fantasizing in remote island outposts about its almost mythic days of marching through the corridors of power.

Later as a graduate student in a cold northern American city, I lived in a delightful tumbledown rooming house we called Toad Hall. By then one or two men had grown beards, and we often sat in the evenings in the Victorian living room listening to a grad student in political science read from C.P. Snow and J.R.R. Tolkien.

At that time the pundits still anticipated that the "corridors of power" world was the world of the future. It was a time of the "end of ideology" and the beginning of an era infused by the Kennedy spirit, enlivened by the ideal of the solution of problems by pragmatic political means. Religiously, we dwelt in the afterglow of the mood of the institutional expansiveness of the fifties. The new element that the great post-sputnik growth of colleges and universities brought with it was enhanced campus ministries and academic departments of religious studies. According to the most-discussed theological book of the day, Harvey Cox's *The Secular City,* religion had to cease its existentialist poses and accept a world in which the traditional experience of the sacred is virtually gone. Now reality is the whine of world-encircling jets, the crackling conversations of teams of experts solving problems, and the hum of multitudes who are not lonely but liberated in tall modern cities. Religious passion in those days could at best be expended in support of "Freedom Rides" and Martin Luther King.

It was in that civil rights movement, though, that America saw, visibly isolated within itself, a class experiencing a different history, set of symbols, inner vision, and commitment from that of the majority culture. These people included the nonviolent but crusading blacks and, in a somewhat different way, their socially-conscious white supporters. The self-imposed inner exile of the white supporters was perhaps most important for the future of pop culture. It is in such separated-out groups that new things can quietly gestate.

Then, suddenly, it happened. Where for a few summers there had been a moral-political movement of people who dressed in white shirts and ties there was now a whole new pop culture. It exploded in San Francisco, in Greenwich Village, on campuses across the country. A new kind of person, almost it seemed a new species, walked the streets. With the swagger of corsair voyagers from Xanadu abruptly disembarked in our drab cities, they flaunted their vivid red, purple, and green paisley shirts, their sandals and buckskins, their hair and headbands, their tinted glasses, even their bizarre gold-painted eyelashes. They dwelt in gypsy-gay flats furnished mostly with huge posters exfoliating startling surreal dreamlike scenes and cloths of India bright as jewels. Incense hung in the air; from stereos came the sound of the dulcet or the hard rhythms of rock music.

They believed they had a vision so new as to make them a new people, the children of a new dispensation. The civil rights movement had in part given them the sense of being a generation apart with a special set of values. But psychedelic drugs were what brought them over Jordan into a new vision of God. The drug experience was the sacrament which bound together the new culture with a sense of community. It gave them the experience of a reality seen as supremely valid, even by those who rarely or never took drugs: a timeless now, infinitely deep and rich in texture, ineffable glory.

The essential quest was inner, though it implied a social utopianism. The goal was not reformism; it was the creation of a new society with a new religion and political structure. One summer, these "children," born at the end of the mythic Second World War and dressed with a childlike gaiety, called to the young of the nation to come to the city of the Golden Gate, turn on, know the cosmos in their heads, live in love, and scatter flowers. In the spring of 1967, the *San Francisco Oracle* —then the most mystical and beautiful and incomprehensible of all the new culture papers and later revived for a while as an underground Christian sheet—published a letter from the "Council for a Summer of Love in the City of San Francisco," dated May 13, 1967.

> TO SONS, TO DAUGHTERS, TO MANKIND, AND TO ALL THE WEAVINGS OF LIFE'S GLORIOUS LOOM: IN THIS MOMENT OF GREATEST NEED FOR TRUE COMMUNICATION, MAY THE FATHER OF ALL PEOPLE AND ALL THINGS

GUIDE US, AS HIS HUMBLE SERVANTS, IN A DEEP UNDERSTANDING OF ONE ANOTHER.

This summer, the youth of the world are making a holy pilgrimage to our city, to affirm and celebrate a new spiritual dawn. I am here as a representative of the Summer of Love. The Summer of Love is a family, and a seed-bearer. We carry to you this message:

The activity of the youth of the nation which has given birth to Haight-Ashbury is a small part of a worldwide spiritual awakening. Our city has become the momentary focus of this awakening. The reasons for this do not matter. It is a gift from God which we may take, nourish, and treasure.

The facts are these: many thousands of young people, our children, our brothers, and our sisters, will soon arrive in this city. *They seek meaning* ...

Already, individuals and groups who have seen deeply into the situation are making preparations. Kitchens are being made ready. Food is being gathered. Hotels and houses are being prepared to supply free lodging. The Council for a Summer of Love expects to receive a huge tent, larger than a football field, which will be put up by the Haight-Ashbury community, and will be open all summer. It will contain a field kitchen, sleeping facilities, educational programs, concerts, art shows, lectures, and similar activities ...

There will be small centers for meditation and discussion, and there will also be large festivals, such as the festival for the Summer Solstice, for Midsummer's Day, the Tolkien Festival of Elves and Hobbits, the Holy Days of the traditional religions, festivals of Christ, and festivals of Krishna, festivals of the young and festivals of the old, festivals of brothers ...

I invite all the world spiritual leaders, all great teachers, all gurus, and all men of enlightenment and good will, to join us in our holy convocation; to come to our blessed city to walk among the youth, to teach those who need, and to learn from those who can give to them.

Second, I announce that the people of Haight-Ashbury and their brothers of Marin and Sonoma counties are preparing a gift for the City of San Francisco. There is a beautiful statue of Saint Francis, located in Marin County, and carved from a holy California Redwood tree. This statue is twenty feet tall.

We are now collecting money to buy this statue. It will be brought by hand or cart across the Golden Gate Bridge in a mighty procession of children and it will be given to the city to be placed in Golden Gate Park at the foot of Haight Street facing East toward the place of Dawn. ...

Little of this, of course, actually happened. But as nothing else a passage like this catches the childlikeness, the poignant idealism, the sense of a new called-out community of those days.

A few statistics, however, may be helpful in assessing the dimensions of the new youth culture, even though fundamentally it was a subjective rather than a statistical revolution.

According to the *Gallup Opinion Index* (Report No. 48, June 1969), of a sample of college students polled, 22 percent had tried marijuana, 10 percent had tried barbituates, and 4 percent had used LSD. This survey did not, of course, touch the nonstudent core population of "full-time" counter culture people who were dwelling in Haight-Ashbury, on beaches, in communes, or in Greenwich Village—the "street people" among whom drug use figures would soar far higher.

The size of the new youth culture was swelled by the marked upsurge in the number of young "runaways." In 1966, as it was really getting underway, 90,246 juvenile runaways were arrested by U.S. officers, a figure up 10 percent from the previous year. The number was up to 170,000 by 1968. Doubtless several times that number were returned home—or returned on their own, or simply disappeared—without federal intervention. Arthur Blessitt estimated that in those years there were at least 500,000 runaways annually—a body of people greater than the populations of Alaska, Vermont, Nevada, or Wyoming—who fled to places like Haight-Ashbury in San Francisco, Greenwich Village in New York, the Sunset Strip in Los Angeles, or Peachtree Street in Atlanta, and were mostly initiated into the "drug culture."[3]

In the same years, church attendance in the U.S. fell from 49 percent during an average week in 1955 to 40 percent in 1971. The fact that this figure fell steadily by a percent a year all through the sixties, both in the years the press talked of drugs, eastern religions, and the "death of God," as well as during the years they reported on the Jesus movement and Christian revival, helps put the latter in perspective. The Jesus movement is of cultural interest, but it seems unlikely to be of great statistical importance. Despite the movement, a campus survey by Daniel Yankelovich, Inc. in 1971 showed that two-thirds of all students rejected organized religion as an important value in a person's life, an increase of 7 percent over 1969. The main difference between 1969 and 1971 is that students in 1971 were just as dissatisfied with American life—"the system"—as in 1969, but they were more cynical about the possibility of effecting change and so were more concerned with finding happiness and meaning in their personal lives. This is the psychic ground out of which the Jesus movement has grown, but it is not true that more than a small percentage has taken that route. Although the Jesus movement is significant in nonstatistical ways, it should be realized that even if it has "converted" several hundred thousand people—the most extreme and probably most exaggerated estimate then given by movement enthusiasts—that was less than one half of 1 percent of the U.S. population and would not be enough to modify the declining church attendance figure of 1 percent (over two million people) a year, which continued until 1972.

To understand what was really going on, though, we must also look at U.S. Census Bureau figures for population by age groups for these years. The July, 1967, estimates are sufficient for our purposes.

15–19 years old: 17,868,000
20–24 years old: 15,197,000
25–29 years old: 12,118,000
30–34 years old: 10,975,000

In comparing the first and last figures, we are really comparing the number of teenagers at the height of the psychedelic explosion with the number in 1952, the year Eisenhower was elected president. We can understand why that rather staid generation would feel not only puzzled, but also swamped, by the rumblings of their replacements. No generation representing such a marked population bulge could fail to have some strong sense of being different and anointed, with special power to shape the future. No society could absorb without some pains of adjustment such a large input of new adults. Add to that the social background of the civil rights movement and the unpopular Vietnam War, which tended to discredit the procedures and values of the Establishment, and we might finally conclude that the passage of that tumultuous and colorful decade was easier rather than more difficult than might have been expected.

But statistics cannot really tell us the meaning of a pop culture movement. It is not evident how many people took drugs only once or twice as a lark and how many were deeply committed to the values of the new drug culture. On the other hand, many who seldom or never took drugs were oriented in important ways to its values. Some, sharing essentially the same world view, preferred alternative means of getting to the same consciousness: yoga, meditation, "growth centers," the "human potentials movement," sensitivity exercises. Almost from the beginning, strong counter currents in these directions raced through the culture, claiming many who rejected the drug scene and its social ramifications as undesirable.

These worlds, however, were continuous with the drug world in that they shared the same presupposition: *reality is known by unleashing subjectivity to its highest ratio.* And in a different way, hundreds of thousands of young people across the country, in small southern and midwestern towns, who were far removed from the new culture's community life and may have been uninitiated into drugs, listened with great common feeling to rock music on the radio and possessed, as flags of remote allegiance, a psychedelic poster or two. In some inarticulate corner of his or her soul, a young man or woman geographically isolated still felt the Beatles and the serious soldiers of the new culture expressed a mood or a yearning he or she had also felt.

Expressions in visual and musical art are the most universal vehicles of communication in most cultures. Innumerable people may participate somewhat in a culture's vision through these means who otherwise have little share in its community and initiatory aspects. A tantalizing hint of transcendental calm may glint from an image of the Buddha or an echo of triumph from a Christian hymn, even to those who have never meditated or been brought over deep waters by Christ. So did the music and art of the psychedelic culture impart to many mostly outside of it something of its mind-bending fascination.

But it is the central initiatory experience which tells the most about a religious vision. The timeless hours of the LSD experience have a structure which Timothy Leary interpreted by means of the scenario of the *Tibetan Book of the Dead,* with its journey of the soul after death through the "bardo" state of glorious and monstrous images created out of the soul's own mind, followed by the delicate and painful reentry into a womb. The LSD experience has also been described as humorous, absurd, or terrifying. Usually no doubt all these elements are present in some manner, and behind them all looms a realization that the cosmos has a wondrous base not quite solidified enough for ordinary perception. For the psychedelic generation, as for Plato, philosophy began with wonder and dealt with what is timeless, the ground of wonder. But the object of wonder was fantasy as well as nature—for all that the mind imagines is equally "real"—and the experience which may be the wellspring of philosophy can be induced through the minutest quantity of a chemical.

The acid "trip" typically begins with cheerful conversation, growing gradually livelier and more incoherent. The experience then turns inward; the most ordinary object may shine out like a supernova with inner splendor. One may pick up a long-awaited letter and, marveling at the luminous colors on the postage stamp, forget to open it. Colored glass, paintings, and flowers come to life, glowing and breathing as though pulsating with deep fires. If the vision turns inward, landscapes may arise before the mind's eye of a magnificence akin to an oriental heaven: soaring cliffs, foaming oceans, trees and birds of paradise, incredible towers and palaces. The experience may then reach a pitch of ecstasy—or it may release deeply disturbing dissociation, a feeling of being lost and unable to cope.

Through LSD the marvels of the "antipodes of the mind," the eternal fountainheads of myth and fairy tale and fantasy, were made potentially available to everyone—or so the drug culture apologists said. "Better living through chemistry!" It was the apogee of pop culture made possible by science: the most grandiose fantasies—or realities—immediately presented on demand after swallowing a pill or eating a dot on a piece of paper. But because this route to "accessible fantasy" was mostly restricted to one age group, was illegal, and because that demographically distinct group had already come to think of itself as separate and slightly accustomed to illegality through the civil rights movement, it remained in an alienated segment of the population. They were initiated, "blew their minds," and suffered the consequences—alone. The symbolic externalia, the visible and conceptual extensions of the vision, both marked them off and communicated something of what they had seen to the outside world.

During the heyday of this culture, I once spent an evening in a large old house in which several young people lived semicommunally. The central figure in the group was an individual with some underground fame as a "hippie astrologer." Like Lucian in Apuleius' *Metamorphoses,* he had undergone a powerful initiatory experience one night on a beach, and there he had received his call to astrology. He had dark brown shoulder-length hair and a full beard, and loved to wear a white robe of raw silk. He looked amazingly like a movieland version of a certain well-known first century figure.

He prepared elegant and expensive astrology charts which were delivered to the client personally, with a long oral interpretation. The consulting room was fragrant with incense and decorated with paisley cloth. The floor was covered with cushions for sitting. The interview opened with a reverent reading of the I Ching. During the many parties in this house, an automatic slide projector would bespangle the wall with colored astronomical photographs—galaxies, nebulae, comets—blazing through the heavy pot smoke. The astrologer would frequently inaugurate the evening with a public lecture, his soft deep voice "rapping" of houses, trines, and nodes. His face was young yet lined, his dark eyes wide, luminous, mystical, and understanding. He was one of those, remarkably frequent in those days, who despite great youth and scant appreciable experience in this lifetime, seemed quietly to comprehend everything. An "old soul" . . . a magus briefly in our midst.

The house was inhabited by a more or less permanent population of six or eight people, and there were always countless "crashers," guests, and clients drifting in and out, all young, all in "hip" attire. In the kitchen, which would never have passed a government health inspection even in west Afghanistan, a huge kettle of soup was always boiling, and there was French bread, wine, and brownies. Among the residents was one young man who never spoke and sat staring endlessly, eyes fixed on some wonder or terror in space beyond our ken: he had had a "bad trip." He was kindly taken care of by the others. Innumerable cats and kittens wandered the house and garden, loved and well-fed, albeit flea-ridden. The walls were hung with pictures of fierce Tibetan gods and enigmatic serene Buddhas, mournful Christs and astrological charts—the symbols of a separate community with a separate reality.

PSYCHEDELIC CULTURE AND JESUS CULTURE

Let us now summarize the major characteristics of the psychedelic culture of the late sixties. We can then compare its presuppositions with those of the Jesus movement, the next image to move across the screen of popular culture.

1. Psychedelic experience defined the fundamental vision of reality. Absolute reality was held to be most amenable to visual images, but was beyond verbal, spatial, or temporal categories. It was splendor and play, without stain or purpose except as introduced by faulty vision. Human nature was seen as psychosomatic; changes in diet, posture, or chemistry can validly change subjective vision, and vice versa. *The Tibetan Book of the Dead* was well chosen by Timothy Leary as a vehicle for interpreting the psychedelic world view. The ultimate vision is of the Clear Light of the Void, in which the dance of atoms and galaxies vibrates continuously and ecstatically. Between it and the viewer march cosmic splendors and monsters, guardians locked in deep sexual union with wisdom, which really come out of the mind.

2. Therefore, subjectivity was the key to reality. Direct awareness of the ultimate vision was, through chemistry and meditation techniques alike, remarkably accessible. Because the means to attainment was through "cleansing the doors of perception," awareness was a matter of adjusting mental faculties within, rather than of external empiricism or deduction. As always, tool and data were mutually limiting. The process, and the mental screen, were identified with the object of the quest. The external cosmos was, therefore, not dead but ecstatic cosmic consciousness waiting to be joyfully joined, in a flash like the union of sperm and ovum, to the clean liberated human consciousness.

3. The goal of life was the "high." The "high" state, so like Abraham Maslow's "peak experience," blissful, creative "being," without any sense of deprivation, lack, or need outside itself, was on these premises sense of deprivation, lack, or need outside itself, was on these premises the only meaningful condition. The drug or meditation state was idealized to deliver this consciousness.

4. **Related modes of expression—art, music, the light show, and crafts—were all centered around the induction of this "high" or were at least reminders of its possibility.** The ethos and "newness" of the culture was exemplified in its art. Posters, crafts, poetry, dress, and above all music, made art bend and twist ordinary perception to imitate or record a drug trip. The smallest bead was a keyhole vision of paradise. Through various media art battered the ordinary channels of perception with hard rhythms, lightning-like flashes, curves and colors. Or, it suggested the edenic paradisical simplicity of nonmaterialistic living. All was nonclassical, noncognitive, noncivilized—a radical neoromanticism. While the new art had some background in art nouveau, the African beat of jazz, and nostalgia for American Indians, or India, it was all mulled in a new wine, inspired by psychedelic experience, and it cumulatively created the pop insignia of a new community.

5. **This generation had a sense of belonging to a new era.** The "Aquarian Age" motif, derived significantly from an arcane astrological datum, typifies the widespread apocalyptic sense of moving through a radical disjuncture of history. A group self-aware of being the firstfruits of a new age, and full of optimistic expectations in the midst of the old, is bound to have a tight community sense.

6. **There was a new relationship to the cosmos.** The new vision and subjectivity led inevitably to a belief that man is not really a freak of nature who somehow has a brain, lost in a dead and pointless universe of matter. He is not *meant* to be an exploitative outsider, as occidental thought is prone to assume, entitled to wrestle with matter and lower life to mold the world for his comfort. Instead man's consciousness is, on its deepest levels, at one with the nonmaterial ground of the universe. While this intuition is not alien to philosophic idealism East and West, it received vigorous new experiential and symbolic support in the new culture. If "everything is alive" and bursting with glorious subjective meaning, then new rationales are given the ancient symbol systems of astrology, magic, polytheism, and the Eastern religions—and these anti-Puritans did not shrink from symbols—which inhere in a vision of the moods of the human mind as continuous with the shifting life of the macrocosm.

7. **This led to a reaction against science and technology.** Those bulwarks of the current American Establishment were held to rest upon a view of man's relation to the cosmos wholly at odds with that of the new subjectivity. Rather than seeking to exploit a "dead" world with analytic, discursive knowledge and ruthless technique, man should find his

modest ecological niche and live harmoniously in it, exploring love and subjectivity. The new community sought to do this through such means as communes, vegetarianism, and organic farming.

8. Even more fundamental was a reaction against history. In 1969 I taught a university class called Mysticism in World Religions. As might be expected, the class attracted a good number of students who strongly identified with counter culture attitudes. When they selected topics for individual reports, I was surprised to find that nearly all chose something from one of two areas: mystical phenomena in prehistoric religion, such as shamanism; or something very current, like mysticism and drug experience, research in parapsychology, alpha waves, and so forth. Very few took a historical topic in "classical" mysticism either East or West. Eckhart, St. John of the Cross, and Shankara were ignored. When I commented on this in class, many said in effect, "We don't like history." History, and preoccupation with the study of history and the experiencing of time as historical, have, to them, led mankind to an impasse. We can now escape our Western bondage to history, though, by going back again to the primordial beginnings of the human saga and finding out from what kind of spiritual consciousness man came. Or again, we can regard the past as utterly different from the present, stop the clocks, and begin anew, new men in a new time. Either way, the attitude was expressive of an apocalyptic, pop culture approach to time and its meaning in human experience.

9. Eastern religions, and the western occult tradition, were popular. These differ from the normative Judaeo-Christian tradition fundamentally in their concept of the meaning of time for spiritual life. Judaeo-Christian time is linear. Where one is in the time stream—whether he is after or before Moses or Christ—is crucially determinative for the nature of his spiritual life. In the East and the alternative Western tradition, all time is like the rim of a wheel, with all points in equal relation to the center. From any point, without much regard for your place in history, you can leap toward the center through eternally available subjective means. Apocalyptic time, postulating an imminent end of history and the beginning of a new world in which all the promises of the Eastern view will be immediately available, has ties to both. But because the apocalyptic was only, as it were, the promise of things hoped for, the new culture generally presumed the Eastern view to be really valid all the time and the basis of any kind of time. It obviously fit in well with the drug experience. Hence, the language and symbols of Eastern religions and occultism seemed strikingly expressive to many.

10. All the foregoing led to a new politics. This was a second stage in the movement, but it came very fast, as did all the culture's metamorphoses. The ramifications of the American counter culture movement vided mysticism-based symbol systems for everything antiestablishment from nature poetry to divination to revolutionary secret societies. As soon as the new American counter culture identified itself and realized that the older culture was not going to vanish like frost before the morning sun, an apocalyptic, mystical desire to accomplish change by revolutionary political means charged it. Revolution has its euphoria, its sense of moral righteousness, its mystical romanticism, its symbols, its apocalyptic stoppage of time. Sharing the antihistorical and antirational spirit of the general culture, the new politics—whether pro-McCarthy or "Yippie"—had a different spirit from the old. It seemed to expect that a single decisive blow, if fired by a pure and uncompromised new consciousness, could vanquish the past and inaugurate the new age. Its characteristics were concentration on a small number of emotionally powerful issues connected with lifestyle values rather than party politics in the ordinary sense. The "new politics," then, was essentially a symbolic crusade expressive of the sense of alienation of a minority group with a different cosmic vision, expressing itself through alternative means as well as ends.

11. It was a movement based in urban society. It is interesting to reflect that most real mystical movements have originated in urban settings or in urbanizing societies. As population pressure builds up in a few centers, a loss of historical consciousness and an interest in the timeless mystical quest often surfaces and spreads. Think of Alexandria or Loyang, Vanarasi and the Ganges Valley in the days of the Buddha, mercantile Flanders and north Germany at the end of the Middle Ages for examples.

The great monotheistic religions with their linear concept of time flourish in pastoral and imperial societies—ancient Palestine, Iran, Arabia, modern Britain, Germany, and frontier America—where there is a low population density and/or room for extensive mobility and expansion in geographical space. This situation creates an awareness of linear, historical time—a sense of concomitant room for expansion in time.

But population crowding creates (a) a turning of expansiveness towards the discovery of "inner space" and (b) a nostalgia for an idealized image of rural society oriented toward cosmic time. A true archaic hunting and agricultural society does not so much produce real private mysticism as a corporate psychic life measured by seasonal labors and festivals. But urban man, yearning for the archaic sense of place and destiny, strives to recover it through attitudes of private mystical identity with nature, the gods, and the All. Or, as in the city-based Christianity of the imperial Roman world and the contemporary Jesus movement, he may perpetuate pastoral, historical-minded symbols, but put his real emphasis on using them to induce an experiential and apocalyptic stoppage of time.

The modern city is both the culmination of history and the subjective end of history. Its hyper-effective communications systems push even the elite into the non-historical, apocalyptic world of pop culture. All images are immediately available—whether you want them or not. The defensive discovery of the subjectivity the city generates often produces a discovery of the mind's lack of rapport with clock time or event time. It is significant that the seed centers of the new culture were in the hearts of the great cities and that most of its adherents came out of urban society, for all their idealization of India and the edenic bower. For that matter it was also evident that it was largely an affluent, middle-class family life which offered the leisure and confidence of security which made disdain of material goods and middle-class values possible. Few blacks or really poor people were found in the counter culture, just as few were people of rural background.

Another aspect of this is that in affluent cities methods of childraising tend to shift dramatically from restrictive to permissive. The person who bears within him memories of a childhood of idyllic freedom will retain favorable images of the happy child's "panerotic," magical and delighted view of the world and a feeling that childhood attitudes and behavior produce good results associated with love and security. Such a person is prepared for the immediacy of images and gods in pop culture.

In pastoral, frontier, and "work ethic" societies, on the other hand, childhood is restrictive, oriented toward deferred reward ("wait until you're older"), and the association of love and freedom with adult manhood. Permissiveness is closer to the usual method of oriental societies; small children often have light discipline and an almost erotic relationship to their mothers, but as they grow older freedom is severly restricted by the patriarchal family or caste system. Significantly, in both cases the image of God is associated with the area of greatest freedom in the scenario of one's life. In the East, it is associated with the mystical subjective expansiveness of the paradise of the womb or the maternal breast, or the boy Krishna's idyllic garden, or the magical omnipotence of gods and bodhisattvas. In the historical Judaeo-Christian tradition, with its pastoral-imperial heritage, one has a contractual, verbal, interpersonal relation to God, like the relationships between adults in the world of trade, marriage, and responsibility. But in our day, many have left the world of that God and made Hermann Hesse's paradigmatic Journey to the East, seeking not only the geographical East but also the sunrise inner East of lost childhood and ultimate origins.

brought up in the new cities merely to act out a secular version of frontier spirituality. This psychology of seeking and bringing out the inner child was perhaps the deepest motif of the new culture, deeper even than the drug experience which gave it experiential and symbolic consolidation. The belief that if one is to look for God, he must look within, can be criticized philosophically. But what is significant is that in the new culture with all its spiritual concern that premise was simply taken for granted. It made God himself "accessible fantasy."

At any rate, the culture had a great number of facets and went through rapid changes. In 1966–67 it was the Flower Children. By 1968 many of them had taken off for rural communes, and many of those left in the cities had become radically political. The political surge culminated with the McCarthy campaign. The disappointment its failure produced, viscerally expressed in the formation of the "Yippies" and the Chicago riots of 1968, was a more traumatic shock than most outsiders realized. Yet that wing of the "movement" suffered another equally battering blow in the upheaval following the Cambodia invasion and the Kent State shootings in 1970. After these events the new community felt futile, depressed, and oppressed. Not only was it politically frustrated; by then it was apparent that its utopian communal dreams had ended in squalor, bitterness, and economic failure augmented by violent opposition from without. The "drug scene" and the "crashing" districts of runaways were riddled with disease, psychological wreckage, crass exploitation by racketeers, perverse kinds of occultism, and despair. The new heaven had become a hell.

Yet it must be appreciated that the new community was still subjectively a community. None could have gone through what they had gone through, have dreamed their dreams and suffered their reversals, and be the same person he would have been had he, like the prodigal's brother, stayed home and never gone to seek the far country. Home answers could never satisfy all that he was now. But the community desperately needed a new identity, a symbol beyond the flower. It needed a flower that had been greatly disillusioned and had greatly suffered, yet could not say its dreams were worthless and should have never been. It wanted a God that as "accessible fantasy" was still accessible.

Christianity emerged out of once pastoral Judaism in an urban milieu, that of the Greco-Roman world. That too was a society of much desperation, of many shattered messianic dreams, and of much idealism and mysticism that never seemed to deliver all it promised. We can compare it to the present-day milieu.

One fall evening in 1971, I visited a prayer meeting and Bible class in the Jesus People House in Hollywood. The small room was packed with "street people" in torn levis and fringed jackets. Girls wore long patterned pioneer woman skirts. Boys and girls alike bore the young-old, too fresh or too creased, faces of their generation.

The meeting opened with a series of lively hymns to guitar accompaniment. The leader suggested some Bible camp variations, hand gestures, and simple part singing, which were enthusiastically received. Next was a session of prayer. Anyone who felt moved to pray interjected, usually in hesitant stumbling phrases, his petitions. Some expressions seemed to be almost ritualized, such as "just now do this," "we come to you." I heard prayers for people who were ill, having a bad time with drugs, separated by military duty, in need of conversion. One worker for the House thanked God for the rapid growth of the movement in Scandinavia, as evidenced by their mail. Another, a tall sensitive young man, gave thanks for the healing of his pet cat. The prayer period ended fervently with a deep wordless ululation, a long chant rising and falling like the sea which broke here and there into individual words of praise or thanks.

The actual Bible class was led by a muscular middle-aged worker from a missionary organization. He sat on the floor leaning against the wall and spoke about the call of Moses from herding sheep to lead the Israelites out of Egypt. The discourse was interrupted by a group of three Jesus musicians in long hair and flak jackets, their guitar cases ornamented with Jesus stickers and crosses. They insisted on being allowed to sing some songs the Lord wanted them to sing just then; in a little while they would have to move on. They sang them, mostly conventional gospel songs. One boy, however, sang a piece he had written himself called "The Church Song," a scathing satire of the socialite church and the prevarications of liberal preachers, contrasted with the accepting openness and certainties of the Jesus people.

When the leader was able to return to his topic, he emphasized that God's call to Moses to come from tending of sheep to do his great work was typical of God. He likes to "reach for the bottom of the barrel." It was the same way with Jesus and with the early church. Despised and rejected people, the offscouring of the earth, were picked by God to confound the wise. The biblical God does not do his work on earth through a brahmin caste, or a spiritual elite of mighty adepts. With true omnipotence he chooses men and communities which seem unsuitable and unworthy.

I looked at the serious and intent faces of the listeners and realized many understood what he was saying. Suddenly, I had a flash of insight into the appeal of the Jesus movement. They too, these street people, consciousness or of the "greening of America," had been treated like the bottom of the barrel, like rejects and outcasts.

It is not necessary to show in detail how the culture of 1967 had failed. Most other movements, including Christianity, have failed in history if judged by their greatest hopes and ideals. The point is that what was needed was a religion for a situation of failure.

It was the evangelical form of Christianity that seemed best able to meet the need of that dark hour for that community. Evangelicalism has a long history of providing identification and meaning in failure situations, of affording a means of spiritual consolidation for "reject" communities, and of being a major folk religion or pop culture symbol system in America (as we shall see in the next chapter).

While the evangelical Jesus movement may superficially seem a reversal of the new culture, it also has strong points of continuity with it. The seeming suddenness and extremism of the reversal is an important point. It fits in with the subjective apocalyptic, conversion psychology of evangelicalism as pop culture.

At the beginning of this chapter, we observed that pop culture is not bound by logical or historical gradualism, but likes to see itself as shifting in mood with the abruptness of dreams or changing television channels. It is an expression of the timeless power the psyche feels beneath the level touched by books or reason. To be able to go from James Bond to psychedelia, and from psychedelia to Jesus, gives a feeling of radical freedom.

But actually the transition from psychedelia to Jesus was not as radical as it seemed on the surface—or to the converted. Actually only one or two variables are involved in the reversal. Most of the characteristics of the psychedelic culture we have listed are also characteristic of evangelicalism and have been carried over into the Jesus movement.

1. For evangelicalism, more than many other forms of religion, subjectivity is the key to reality. The living presence of Jesus must be experienced within; this is its key principle of validation.
2. The goal of life is a "high"—the joyous assurance of knowing Jesus.
3. Expression through music is central to evangelicalism and so are the visual symbols of the Bible, carried about, read, and venerated, and to a lesser extent the cross. Reference to an idealized rural past, the days of the "old-time religion," is as important as the communalistic edenism of the psychedelic culture.
4. Evangelicals have always possessed a sense of belonging to a separated culture, one which is a firstfruits of a New Age, when

the Gospel will be spread throughout the world (the this-worldly hope) and Christ will return (the supernatural hope).

5. Evangelicalism, with its heritage of fundamentalist belief in biblical miracles, biblical literalism, and separation from worldly culture, has been in long-standing tension with science and technology, just as the counter culture has. The biblicism of the Jesus people represents a point of continuity as well as of discontinuity with the non-Christian counter culture. Leslie Fiedler pointed out, in a lecture to the Congress of Learned Societies in the Field of Religion in 1972, that one characteristic of the counter culture was a recovery of the experience of reading selected books as *scripture*, rather than simply for "cultural enrichment" in the humanistic sense. The ordinary middle-class home today may have shelf after shelf of "great books," book club books, coffee table books. The back-to-nature communard may not have such works and may disdain them. But it is not true that these folk do not read. Instead they have a slim but well-worn library of a few books read, not for culture, but as guides to salvation: the *Tibetan Book of the Dead,* the *Whole Earth Catalog,* Tolkien's *The Lord of the Rings,* Hesse, Heinlein's *Stranger in a Strange Land.* These books are read as the old Puritans read Milton, Bunyan, and the Bible—as explanations of visions and of the deepest tumults of the soul, as guideposts on the Way, almost as incantations to create alternative worlds. The Jesus people read in the same way, but their shelf is even narrower: the Bible, usually the King James Version, as the one authentic oracle (One Way!), two or three received commentaries—Hal Lindsey's *The Late Great Planet Earth,* and a fundamentalist exegesis or two. All these works are read not as literature or for their stylistic power, but as simple, straight manuals of the way things really are, as guidebooks to an invisible reality.

6. In the same way, evangelicalism shares with the new culture a suspicion of history, holding that the essential events and authority—the saving work of Christ, the Bible—are in a separate lasting category from the rest of human history. History's account is deeply tinctured with illusion; the study of history is suspect if it threatens biblical infallibility. The much castigated "higher criticism" is also in that category.

7. The political role of evangelicalism in America, best exemplified in the nineteenth century abolitionist and the twentieth century prohibition movements, has much in common with the "new politics" of the counter culture. Both were oriented toward a very small number of issues rather than to party politics and the control of the ordinary functions of government. Both provided a political-social symbol for people who shared a common sense

powerful issues connected with life style values, expressed politically the sense of nostalgia for an earlier time when life was presumably simpler and more integrated, with less disparity between religious, personal, and social values. In short politics becomes crusade rather than political technology.

8. Regarding the matter of urban versus rural roots, we may observe that while American evangelicalism came out of the frontier and has virtually a folk religion status in some rural areas, its most spectacular achievements in the last hundred years—the evangelistic campaigns of Dwight L. Moody, Billy Sunday, and Billy Graham, the present Jesus movement—have been in the large cities. Their rhetoric, like that of the counter culture, indicated an obvious appeal to the problems of subjectivity and the nostalgia for an idealized rural milieu which haunt the urbanite.

In all of these areas, there is a continuity between the present Jesus movement and traditional evangelicalism and between both of them and the new culture. Particularly to be emphasized are the roles of proselytizing and music in this three-way continuity, less obvious factors perhaps than such clear points of contact as subjectivity, alienation, apocalyptic hope, and nostalgia, but for that reason significant clues. Proselytizing and music are points of continuity in the realm of outward expression and so suggest similarities in the social and inward essences of the movements.

Proselytizing refers to the aggressive act of "selling" a belief. It implies the use of emotional, high-pressure rhetoric, advertising, and, especially, directing appeals for conversion and conviction personally to individuals with overtones of acceptance or rejection of the "seller," with whom the person is in a charged, face-to-face relationship individually or as a member of an audience. Sometimes religions are content to practice their faith quietly without attempting to win others. Sometimes they adopt only a soft-spoken outreach, and sometimes they proselytize vigorously. The option selected says much about the nature of the group and its experience. The Jesus movement, traditional evangelicalism, and the counter culture religious causes have shown a strong tendency toward proselytizing, in contrast to liberal Protestantism or ethnic religions like Greek Orthodoxy. In the case of the counter culture religions, one thinks of Nichiren Shoshu, Krishna Consciousness, Scientology, the Maharishi's Transcendental Meditation Movement, and of course the fervor with which some advocates of drug-induced ecstasy, like Timothy Leary, tried to persuade others to "turn on, tune in, drop out." But older styles of counter culture religiosity, like the Zen of the "beatniks," were much less aggressive.

Under what conditions do groups actively proselytize? It does not appear that strength of conviction, or a particular kind of belief, themselves induce the proselytizing mood. Examples of both static and proselytizing faiths could be produced anywhere along these spectra. Rather, proselytizing seems to be the result of particular kinds of circumstances that cause particular moods and styles to arise in religious persons.

Leon Festinger, Henry W. Riecken, and Stanley Schachter have, in their book *When Prophecy Fails,* provided a splendid study of a UFO group moving from a "closed" to a proselytizing stance.[4] The surprising conclusion, borne out time and again in the history of religion, is that, given real commitment, it is precisely experiences of "disconfirmation" that induce a shift to proselytizing zeal on the part of the believers. Experiences of disappointment, failure, and (to the outsider) discrediting of the religion may lead the believing community to want to convince others of its continuing truth and future hopes.

The group studied in *When Prophecy Fails* had believed, in accordance with psychic messages, that on December 21 of a certain year much of the world would be inundated by a great flood, but that "space brothers" would descend in flying saucers to rescue the members of the cult and other believers. While preparing for this day, members were very hesitant about talking to reporters and other outsiders. On the night of the 20th, they waited up, fully expecting their extraterrestial friends at midnight. When they, and the anticipated holocaust, failed to materialize, there was at first a black hour of grim disappointment. But a new message was received through "automatic writing" which indicated that the faith and spiritual power of this group that night had released such a stream of light into the world that the disaster had been averted. Immediately the mood changed to splendid joy at the wonder of these tidings. The next day they called the reporters to impart this news to the world, and from then on assumed a strongly proselytizing attitude; one member even travelled about the country as a St. Paul of this saucerian faith.

Here, the disconfirmation led to a deep shared experience in the group that designated them as a people set apart in a new way from the outside world. They no longer waited in apocalyptic expectation but enjoyed regenerated subjectivity. Realizing that an invisible but marvelous change had indeed occurred, rather than unbearable disappointment, they had a secret to be shared. Because it was now a subjective realization and a joyful mood, it was in principle available to all and so could be spread by proclamation. Christianity itself, after its initial disappointment that Jesus did not return within the first generation, made a similar transition.

The movement of the new culture from the quietism of Zen to the

The movement of the new culture from the quietism of Zen to the religious proselytizing of psychedelia and new cults, and from the politics of the civil rights movement to the Jesus movement is marked by a series of disconfirmations: the assassination of John F. Kennedy and the death of secular hope which seemed somehow to accompany that tragedy, the failure of psychedelia as a culture, the failure of the McCarthy campaign. Each political-cultural failure induced a subjectivization of the social movement into a religious cause. It was as though to say, "We were right all the time, but it was really a new spirituality we were being set apart for, not a political goal as we thought. Accept *it* and acknowledge we were right."

Just as certain favorite hymns, like "Amazing Grace" and "Jesus, Lover of my Soul," unite all stripes of traditional evangelicals and markedly facilitate the evangelical experience, so rock music unites and facilitates all the spiritual quests of the new culture, from psychedelia to Jesus. A recent movie, "Rainbow Bridge" starring Jimi Hendrix, illustrated this. It was filmed at the Maui Occult Research Center in Hawaii. The young people living at this center talk of many things—drugs, surfing, sex, out-of-the-body experiences, ecology, yoga, meditation, UFOs. A "hip" guru, with long hair and beard, says that he is the Supreme Consciousness experiencing this world through these eyes, but is not these eyes ... They all follow various paths, sometimes arguing over their relative merits.

But the real climax of the picture is a great rock concert. Here, all those who had been on different "trips" come together. One by one, everyone begins dancing the private, orgiastic dances appropriate to such music, and the ecstasy of the music and dance seemed to transcend that of the "trips." The young audience in the Aquarius Theatre on Sunset Boulevard where I saw the movie were obviously pulled into the vortex of rock and clapped spontaneously at the end of each number. Jesus rock, such as the music of Larry Norman, makes a bridge from that world to the Jesus movement.

We must also recognize some differences between the "old" new culture and the Jesus movement. Quite apart from the integrating vision—consciousness-is-all versus the figure of Jesus—some points in our list of characteristics of the new culture have been reversed. Obviously, psychedelic experience does not define the fundamental reality, save that the idea of a "high" as a moment of supreme perception is still the central value and save as some have been brought to Jesus in reaction against psychedelia. The Jesus movement is less multisensory; accepting music and even dance, it rejects meaningful communication through the sense of smell (incense) and to a large extent through the visual sense. There is relatively little important visual expression except in the printed page of the Bible or the tract. Most important of all, the Jesus movement strongly rejects the interest in Eastern or occultist traditions so characteristic of the other new culture.

To this extent the Jesus movement represents a reintegration and resocialization into American life of an element which had been becoming more and more alienated from it. The pendulum swings the other direction. For most people any process of deracination can go only so far; however much one makes a spiritual, cultural, and political excursus from one's culture, one is still tied to it by such fundamentals as geography, language, family, and early education, and sooner or later these elements demand their due. Self-isolation from personal roots is hard to maintain without feelings of guilt and strain. As the excitement of the new wears off, these feelings become more and more powerful. Yet you cannot go home again as though you had never left. Like the Jesus movement evangelicalism has an aura about it of protest and alienation against the sophisticated and elite of America, yet it also has powerful support and cultural roots in America. Thus the evangelical Christ makes the heritage of a culturally Christian nation once more accessible to its estranged children, and makes something of the new counter culture spirituality available to that nation. We must now look more closely at evangelicalism's history and meaning in this nation.

2

Evangelicalism in America

RELIGION ON AMERICAN SOIL

BEHIND THE CONTEMPORARY JESUS MOVEMENT lies the panorama of American religious history. For the historian, nothing is without antecedents. The present movement has special characteristics, but it also presents a phrasing of the evangelical message, and induces experiences of salvation, which have been heard and felt many times before in the leafy woods and on urban streets of our land. The Jesus movement is definitely a new outcropping of that religious force called evangelicalism that has profoundly affected American religious life for many generations. Wherever there is Protestant simplicity, melodious hymns, warm and emotional preaching, and felt personal conversions to Christ, where there are revival meetings and perhaps gifts of the Spirit such as speaking in tongues, where the Bible is believed quite literally and the church tries above all to relive the New Testament, there is evangelicalism.

Americans have always been a religiously diverse people. From its root periods to the present, the country has known the fierce ecstasy of the Indian shaman, the burning glory of Spanish Catholicism, the high-towered romanticism of English and Irish Catholicism, the Quakers' irenic mysticism, Anglican stateliness, Calvinist learning and sobriety,

Lutheran biblical profundity. We have heard the poignant joy of black religion and the ageless calls of the Jewish cantor. On these shores we have long sheltered Deists, atheists, occultists, Spiritualists, mystics, Amish people, Eastern Orthodox, and Buddhists. Neither evangelical Protestantism nor any other faith can claim in any special way to be *the* American religion, or even the religion of the "Founding Fathers."

But evangelicalism has had a special destiny in America. Here "evangelical" does not mean what it does in Germany, where the term generally refers to a state Protestant church. In America evangelicalism is a particular manner of interpreting Christianity. We might almost say it is a particular Christian mood or style, though it also implies a certain doctrinal and psychoexperiential content. It is not a denomination, though it has spawned many and represents a party or school in many others.

But characteristically the evangelical movement is not involved with denominationalism. Its most potent institutions, whether the old-time revival or the coffeehouse of the present Jesus movement, have had few denominational ties and have drawn persons to its central experience from all churches or from none. Evangelicalism's most effective continuing organizations, from the old National Holiness Alliance to the modern Campus Crusade for Christ, have been organized independently of denominations and are cross-denominational in support. Many major evangelical churches and Bible schools are independent.

As a tradition of teaching, mood, and style rather than of an institution, evangelicalism has been close to the mood-conscious, institution transcending world of pop culture. Its traditional role is now represented in the Jesus movement. Along with diluted puritanism and the New Thought or positive-thinking mood, evangelicalism has supplied most of the stock of religious images which appear in American songs, greeting cards, popular art, and literature. These three traditions meet to form pop culture religion, lately augmented by a fourth, the counter culture's occultism. The pop consumer seems, without apparent awareness of any inconsistency, simultaneously at home with salvation by hard work and rigorous morality; salvation by thinking beautiful, "inspirational" thoughts; and salvation by the fervent affective veneration for Jesus and Bible communicated by the beloved old hymns about the cross and the blood. A young modern woman of my acquaintance attends a very traditional Baptist church where she has "accepted Christ," and weeps with feeling as the gospel hymns are sung and converts respond to the altar call, yet she also reads New Thought classics like "Acres of Diamonds," believes strongly in astrology and reincarnation, and every full moon practices a method of meditation promoted by a UFO cult.

However, the special role of evangelicalism has given the history of Christianity in America its distinctive tone. Not always has evangelicalism been merely a part of a general religious potpourri. It has also always had its exclusivist adherents and its centers of monolithic strength. Like all powerful social movements, it has both centrifugal and centripedal force. Its mood, style, and ideas have been diffused into the general cultural stream, as well as pulling people out of the general milieu toward evangelicalism's alternative spiritual world with greater and greater intensity of commitment. Indeed, the soul of evangelicalism has never been completely at peace with "culture." Its ideology has often produced contention and separatism. Bringing not peace but a sword, it has sown bitter division within communities, denominations, and families. For those who have been brought under the power of the evangelical Christ, the personal integration the experience has wrought has far outweighed in importance the integration of family and society. For evangelicalism is above all an individualizing faith which puts getting the person right with God absolutely first. It puts the role of religion in generating integrating personal experiences ahead of the other traditional role of religion—unifying the family and society—if a choice must be made.

Thus while evangelicalism has certainly played a culture forming and culture validating role in America, the means have been through making a certain set of subjective feelings the touchstone of cultural value decisions. Does drinking, or higher education, or exaltation of the Bible reinforce or disenforce personal, subjective integration around a luminous interiorized image of Jesus and the felt power of the Holy Spirit? In this manner, rather than in terms of direct appeals to the value of passive participation in a sacred cultural or ecclesiastical tradition, do questions like these present themselves to evangelicals.

Not for them is the "implicit faith" of the medieval peasant making holy the yearly round through hearing mass on Sundays and holy days, or the way of the tribalist celebrating the sacred king, or the "karma yoga" of the Hindu supporting world order by impersonally observing the usages of his caste. For the evangelical Jesus stands above all of this cultural religion demanding that each individual make a decision for or against him, and personally experience intensely and subjectively his presence and power. Comparatively, evangelicalism is closer to what preceded it on American soil than to the "implicit faith" versions of Christianity. In some Indian tribes it was expected that each young man, and above all each shaman, go into the woods to wait until, after prayer and fasting, he had personally encountered his Guardian Spirit and internalized that great being's power. Both evangelicalism and the

Indian ceremony were religions of psychoexperiential initiation, rather than of classical form.

Because an experience-centered and inherently separatist movement has been a lasting part of the religious landscape in America (it is easy to see why religions centered on inner personal experience tend to fragment), religious life here has been kept active, fluid, individualistic, and pluralistic. Largely because of evangelical yeast, Americans attend church and think about religion more than people of most other advanced nations. For the same reason, religion has provided a different kind of cultural unity than in one-religion or one-church nations. We have been forced to stress the civil values of pluralism—or of what common denominator can be found. Consider the pallor of the language to which American politicians must resort when endeavoring to speak religiously without offending anybody. Yet while evangelicalism can never be *the* religion of America, as the source of much of the culture's religious rhetoric and imagery, it is far more than simply a minority sect.

THE OFFICIAL TEMPLE AND THE SHORT PATH

In all religious cultures there are several strata. Among them we can find illuminating parallels to evangelicalism and even the Jesus movement. First, the great religions of the world all have a majority tradition which is cool, official, and deeply learned. Its rites—the sacrifices of the brahmins, the offerings of the great Roman temples and Shinto shrines, the throngs kneeling in prayer in the monumental mosques of Cairo and Tehran—have an attractive dignity and a sense of age-old tradition. Theirs is the beauty of old chased silver, or of sublime opera.

Within all these traditions, however, are counter movements emphasizing intensity of personal experience more than tradition, scholarship, dignity, or sanction by the elite. Usually appealing most to the outcasts and dissatisfied, these movements say, "We can give *you* directly and intensely what is only hinted at in the official temples. We have a 'short path,' a special plan or technique which can give you right away what would take years and years in the temple. Come out, join us. Our group is made up of nobodies; it is small and disreputable. We are virtually outlaws, but with us you can meet the gods face to face and feel their power. There, at the temple, you only call to them through miles and miles of empty space." So said the Tantrists of India, the Sufis of Islam, the Chinese Taoist adepts, the Mystery Cults of the ancient Mediterranean.

All these counter movements employed special techniques for inducing intense initiatory experiences which reoriented the structure of the psyche by radical means. Drugs, chanting, visualizations, dancing, vertigo, and eroticism have been among the intense stimuli used to trigger a sudden, quick "breakthrough" to a reconstellated psyche.

Evangelicalism makes a similar appeal, couched in Christian phraseology, offering a comparable sudden individual transformation through the "short path" of "accepting Christ" and the power of the Holy Spirit, not in a nominal but in a deeply felt way induced by various means. It has known all the techniques mentioned above except drugs, though the intense arousal of psychic energy necessary to a short path breakthrough experience has been (in contrast to non-Christian short paths) generated principally by intense preaching, hymns, and the use of confrontational psychology. The annals of revivalism, prayer meetings, and evangelical spiritual journals, however, are full of phenomena like dancing, shouting, chanting, visualizations (of Jesus), and overtones suggestive of sublimation of erotic energy.

In any case, the American religious "underground," like that of other cultures, has appealed to those who require a single strong subjective experience, who demand a clear plan to obtain it, and who need the support of a cultus—preaching, hymns, motor expression—centered around the evocation of the experience. Such persons naturally are not satisfied with the major tradition. Its version of the recognition of Deity, however learned and aesthetic, is not really aimed at the same goal at all. It leaves out the person who, because he or she is in the general culture yet senses he or she is not sharing in all its benefits, is divided within himself or herself and in need of deeper subjective integration. Such a person accepts the religious language of the general culture (he or she may not really know any other), but cannot do so completely on the culture's terms. Whether high or low in family status, he or she has been through things which caused a more intense self-discovery.

This person is a Chinese Taoist whose mind wandered during the Confucian rites, an American pioneer who had to fight against the wilderness, a Hindu for whom orthodoxy did not solve the problem of sexuality, an ancient Greek slave uprooted from familiar grove and shrine and left alone spiritually in an alien city. Inwardly, he has lost the calmness which sense of social place bestows; nothing is left but gnawing self-awareness, and a yearning for experience to fill the void. If an intellectual this person might become a mystic or an existentialist. But it is far more likely he will hear the call of those who offer a "short path" to knowing the gods face to face, a far greater thing than knowing even a sacred king.

Usually the "short path" remains the way of an outlaw underground religious minority. But America has been unusually productive of dislocation and individualism in social contexts where (unlike modern Europe) religious language was still quite viable. In some respects, thanks to evangelicalism, it has joined that very small category of societies—Tibet, some primitive tribes, ancient Phrygia—where a "short path," individual-experience-centered approach has paradoxically left its usual underground role and become virtually a major, almost official tradition. In these cases the society has shifted full circle to center around "short path" values as determinative of general cultural values. Makers of popular religious opinion disparage the cool, official, and learned style of most majority forms of religion. Subjective experience becomes not a means of validating protest, but of expressing acceptance of popular culture values.

Such a shift is very difficult to accomplish, since a culture focusing with abnormal one-sidedness on subjectivity becomes as unstable as one which represses it to the point of explosive rebellion. However, the non-evangelical Protestant churches and the Roman Catholic and Jewish traditions have generally remained strong enough to provide a counterweight in America.

Where, as in some parts of the South, evangelicalism is nominally the major tradition, what actually happens is that the production of the "short path" experience, culturally sanctioned, becomes a subjectively felt ritual which integrates persons into the culture. So, like tribal initiations, it is a deeply felt culturally reinforcing experience. Yet the general prestige of emotional, feeling values, of small group loyalty, and of the transformed and sanctified personality typical of "short path" traditions remains, as does the power of rhetoric and singing reminiscent of the "short path" experience.

But no "short path" tradition ever seems to feel secure in the unaccustomed role of dominator of culture rather than of outsider. Even when it seems strong, it still wants to find ways in which its adherents are an alienated minority compared to a larger, materially stronger circle—the South compared to America as a whole, the country against the city, America against an alien world unappreciative of its values. Its rhetoric always seems to bear an edge of defensive wariness, as well as of warmth of in-group and in-self feeling, yet on other occasions its power, numbers, and missionary triumphs are proclaimed almost too loudly. The same style can be detected in Tibetan Buddhism as compared to the rest of Buddhism and the world outside Tibet. So it is with the Jesus movement.

A culture dominated by "short path" values does not, of course, really reinforce individualism as a short path does when it is a minority movement to which the alienated feel called. In fact, even then there is a sense in which the "short path" can only impart conformity to a new personality style traditional to the short path group. The whole point is to lose a former painful individuality in favor of patterned subjectivity integration. In its place feelings and behavior expressive of integration are acquired, and norms characteristic of the group are accepted. Intellectual and emotional diversity are more typical of the "temple" tradition, where only outward conformity is required.

EVANGELICAL TEACHING AND PRACTICE

The basic tenet of evangelicalism is that a person must have a definite, deeply experienced, personal relationship with Jesus Christ. You must believe that, though no longer visible to physical eyes, Jesus is living today as much as ever; that you can know him and talk with him; that he is, moreover, all-powerful; and that you can trust him to answer all your problems in this world and the next, particularly problems of sorrow, emptiness, and the anxiety caused by guilt.

The evangelical believes, with other orthodox Christians, that in his death on the cross Jesus paid a price demanded by God for all the sins of the world. He stresses this atonement by personally affirming—as the keystone of the personal relationship—that the paid price specifically applies to his own sins.

Typically, though not always, evangelicals emphasize that the establishment of the personal relationship with Christ and the acceptance of forgiveness of sins should be attained in a single powerful experience. Whether it is coming forward during an invitational hymn at a church service or revival meeting, or in deep prayer alone, somewhere a person will have his hour with God when he will sense the deep power of the Holy Spirit stir within him and will see the cross before his mystic eyes, and will know that the past is past and all his scarlet sins are made white as snow. The experience is commonly called "being saved" or "becoming a Christian." The literature is full of accounts of them. The evocation of this experience in "sinners"—those who have not had it—is the main purpose of revivals and evangelical preaching. Personal expressions of "accepting Christ" are often quasi-ritualized by such tokens as raising a hand or coming forward. It may also include ecstatic phenomena such as shouting, trance, and uncontrollable tears.

The evangelical does not forget the Christian's life after the initial experience. With the experience or, according to some, in subsequent experiences, comes the power of the Holy Spirit, the Third Person (with God the Father and Jesus Christ the Son) of the triune Christian God. He gives joy and inward guidance ("I've got those Holy Ghost grins") to the believer who has accepted Christ's salvation. For some (the pentecostalists) his presence is made known by "speaking in tongues." Many evangelicals (those in the "holiness" tradition) affirm that after receiving the Holy Spirit, it is possible for the Christian to live, with his help, entirely free from further sin.

Evangelicals have always stressed experience more than forms of church government or sacraments. They do insist on certain points of doctrine: the Trinity, Christ both God and man, the Virgin Birth, the atonement for sin. While not overly preoccupied with philosophical theology, they will attack strongly those they feel to be "watering down" such central doctrines as these. Almost always they affirm vehemently the full verbal inspiration and infallibility of the Scriptures. Although it may have greater or less psychological importance to individual evangelicals, they generally look toward the imminent Second Coming of Christ to judge the world. In this world, which is passing away, they expect frequent signs and wonders of the other world and its power: answer to prayer, guidance, conversion, healing.

Spiritual rebirth, infallible Scripture, signs and miracles, explicit doctrine, and awareness of the approaching End, combine to build around the evangelical a magic circle invisibly cutting him off from those for whom these things have no meaning. Here he lives as in an alternative world. This is no criticism; all persons have made their own world to a large extent, and all religion is grounded in man's hunger for "otherness," for a transition or rebirth to another kind of world, a hunger as biting as hunger for food and sex.

Within the evangelical's magic circle, time moves in a different way. If outside it flows by like a great river too deep and turgid to differentiate, the circle, like a refracting lens, resolves its secret motions into splendid clarity. He sees mighty rocks on the river's bed and the creatures that dwell there; in one place the currents are seen to run with tremendous speed, in another the river stops and appears not to flow at all; in still others it eddies into strange side diversions.

The infallibility of Scripture sets the whole narrative of the Bible, for the evangelical, in a special time capsule. It happened in the course of history, but it has not been borne away on the splashing waves of the river. Instead the Bible and its time stands like a lighthouse in the midst of history. Bible time is special; it stands in equal relation to all other points in time. The evangelical is always contemporaneous with it, particularly with the time of Christ. He always wants to collapse into nothing all time between himself and the New Testament. He strives to negate all customs and attitudes which have evolved in the life of the church between then and now. He wants to walk into the time capsule which is the New Testament world, with its miracles, its expectation of an immediate end, and above all the mighty tangible presence of Jesus Christ. He wants to be the thirteenth disciple and to write in his life the twenty-ninth chapter of the book of Acts. He yearns to merge the magic circle of his own "otherness" world, his alternative reality, with the New Testament time capsule.

Thus Dwight L. Moody, for example, preached on the life of the early church as though the apostles were walking the streets of Chicago or Philadelphia. The evangelical pictures Christ in his mind just as he is presented in the New Testament, walking the hills of Galilee or hanging on the sordid cross outside Jerusalem. He wants to talk with others about Jesus just as did Peter and Paul, without ceremony or equivocation and with the same confident powers of speech and healing hands. He wants his life to be as transformed as those people of long ago called from their nets and tax tables.

But it is no easy thing to move from one world to another, or to jump out of one's native time to make a cathexis with another. I myself was at one time close to an intensely, poignantly romantic Anglo-Catholicism. I dwelt, as an alternative reality, in a fairyland Middle Ages of pilgrimage and piety somewhere between the Seven General Councils of the Church and Lyonesse. This alternative was supported by the whole panoply of Gothic imagination. Ecclesiastical architecture, church ceremonial, vestments, incense, and music were such as to make walking into the churches of this persuasion a sensuous as well as a subjective entry into the portals of our other world.

The evangelical has little support from such externals. He does not wear the clothes, or even sing the nasal tunes, of the first century. He prefers to approximate its reality by wearing what is ordinary today, as the apostles wore what was ordinary then. However, he does not actually escape history because in practice he is strongly affected by the particular form which the Protestant Reformation's rejection of the externalia of medieval Catholicism took.

The evangelical's short path is one of internal, subjective reorientation. A few visual symbols—the cross, the open Bible, flowers—may be present in evangelical churches, but the potent, almost drug-like melodiousness of evangelical hymns (or of modern "Jesus rock") play a virtually indispensable part. They also help to induce what for American evangelicals is a secondary alternative world, that of the early America of frontier revivals and supposed sturdy piety. Preaching and the supportive testimony of others are indispensable props of evangelicalism.

These visual and audio symbols are meant to release great wells of emotional energy sufficient to cause the subjective jump. They make possible the visualizations, the sense of psychic movement, the crossing of the invisible barriers between present and past, and between past sinfulness and future cleanliness, which place the believer marvelously in the time capsule where the luminous Christ stands amidst his disciples.

Deep subjective experience, by which the serpentine muscles of the mind are twisted to another configuration, is necessary just because there is no continuing support for the new world through the primary senses in the way there is in traditions whose worship visibly reenacts an alternative reality. The evangelical must make himself a man of another time while living in this. He must make manifest in his words and manner that he is a man of two realities, the one sovereign over the other. For evangelicals, not only church life and talking about the goodness of the other reality, but also avoidances are signs of detachment from the life of this world. Usually drinking and smoking, and often playing cards, dancing, going to the theatre, and wearing "worldly" clothes, are considered incompatible with "being a Christian."

A very important dynamic of effecting change to the alternative world is what may be called the *confrontational psychology of evangelicalism.* The jump is made, as we have seen, in a single experience comparable to what Buddhists would call "sudden enlightenment" like Zen satori, in contrast to a slow process of psychic rearrangement bit by bit. Those who advocate sudden conversion or enlightenment say that because the alternative reality is a whole world, requiring inner consistency, one is either in it or not. To be in it at all one must have a power which suffices to take the leap in a single bound; you can no more do it in stages than you can cross a chasm in several steps. The leap either takes you to the other side, or you are nowhere.

To this end evangelical rhetoric, whether in sermons or in one-to-one encounters, seeks to focus issues down to stark, black and white dimensions and to create strong psychic energy by raising the emotional tension of encounter to higher and higher intensities. Anger and resentment are better than bland passivity; when any kind of emotional intensity is aroused, it can suddenly change course, go in unexpected directions. Nothing can be done without arousal of energy. Spiritual issues are reduced to one: acceptance or rejection of the "claims of Christ." They are presented with stronger and stronger emotional overtones, whether the mood is fiery and argumentive, soft and poignantly appealing, or joyfully invitational. Put in the context of accepting or rejecting the speaker, sooner or later a crisis occurs for the hearer. He must either accept Christ or end the encounter.

This process is central to evangelicalism. Since it is not supported much by nonverbal signs and symbols, living in the alternative world almost requires verbal communication about it by the believer. The more you talk about the other, biblical-time world, and the more others are brought into it, the more its reality in the present day is reinforced.

The man attracted to a short path is a man of complexity, a person in some ways more complicated, more torn apart by inner conflicts, than the ordinary person of his society. The process of resolving the complexity is not one of simple decomplexification. It is rather one of rearrangement of psychic constituents into a balanced pattern, like a mandala. For the evangelical this means the production of something like a dumbbell-shaped map of the psyche. Everything is grouped around two poles, with a channel of access between them. The two poles are the "world" and the alternative New Testament reality, and the latter is sovereign, the "sovereignty of Christ."

The patterning of complexity is one of individuation, of discovering or creating a viable individual with an inner reality resistant to the chances and conflicts of the outer world. Having an inner reality anchored outside of present time obviously creates a feeling of invulnerability in this world. So does engaging in confrontational dialogue. It means that you are patterning external reality in other people on the basis of your own secret reality, rather than being molded like clay by the outer world. Talking, like singing, is therefore very important to evangelicalism. Through speech we shape the subjective realms out of which speech comes (that is, we believe what we hear ourselves saying) as much as express a content already there. Speech is particularly important to individuation. It is significantly the most important medium in the Semitic religions (Judaism, Christianity, Islam), the religions of highly individualized Western man, insofar as individuation means being able to maintain a separate inner reality in the face of interpersonal encounter. Those religions whose secondary reality is reinforced by visual and sensual media—art, music, sacrament—are closer to a deeper, more tribal, more collective, level of psychic life. Clearly evangelicalism lives importantly on both levels.

However, evangelical man—despite a liking for military and sports imagery—sees religion as highly individual rather than as cosmic or tribal. This is not a categorical matter, as the highly supportive role of the evangelical church demonstrates. But the real locus of the entry into the magic circle is subjective rather than cultic. Christ is a decision one must make as an individual, regardless of how others feel, or so he understands the matter.

The process of individual conversion begins with "conviction of sin." You first become consciously aware of the potential within you for individuation through discovery of the chaotic nature of your complexity. You feel guilt toward your family, your own hopes and ideals, and God. Then evangelical rhetoric sets up the splendor and suffering love of the image of Christ as a contrast. Christ is all that is whole and beautiful, like a mother's arms to a lost child. He is an opposite pole to which you can flee. The intensity of expression raises the spiritual temperature to a point where complexity melts into broad monolithic feelings, which are then polarized: guilt versus Christ. You are made to see you can avoid both the confusion of life and the intensity of the confrontational situation by acceptance of what one who really seems to care wants accepted. You become a Christian.

Some characteristics of evangelical rhetoric: the anxiety of the "lost" state of chaotic complexity is exacerbated by accentuating its natural and supernatural terrors; the corresponding glory of the good is identified with the aesthetic glories of powerful music and heavenly security; the child in every adult, wanting home and mother, is drawn out—the "good" emotions are those simple joys and fears carried over from childhood. The evangelist displays sublime confidence, and becomes the sort of father whose approval everyone wants. Concepts of cleanness and purity are contrasted with words like "filth" and "wallowing." Above all, though, the appeal is to the resolution of inner complexity; you are given "good" and "bad" labels to attach to various parts of your nature or images in your mind to help in that process. All this is simultaneously the strength and weakness of evangelicalism in the modern world.

EVANGELICALISM AND SOCIETY

The complex and ambivalent attitude of evangelicals toward American society as a whole is the result of both a complex history and psychology. The social core of the tradition is the Anglo-Saxon and Scotch-Irish pioneer stock which pushed west from the eastern seaboard to settle the heartland of the nation. Rural folk cut off from urban intellectual centers, they were proud of their individualism and achievements.

They understood the Puritan ideals of hard work and deferred reward. They struggled to clear land, dig out stones, and plant trees for the sake of their old age and their children. They followed a strict moral code in this life for the sake of a heavenly reward in the next. Hard work and deferred reward were interiorized by evangelicalism in the guilt-salvation process and again in the activism characteristic of evangelicals. The evangelical alots a minimum of time to the contemplative enjoyment of his religion, save perhaps in his love of hymns, in favor of the communication process: preaching, talking, praying with more fervor than pleasure, organizing campaigns, reading the Bible and other literature, writing. Precisely because it is a religion of such high individuation, it seems, the evangelical must be regularly finding himself in interpersonal and future-oriented activity—and in self-reinforcement through hearing others talk the same language. It was in this respect, in fact, that most frontier evangelicals differed with the Puritans. The self-reliant frontiersmen thought they should be able to do more, and feel more, about the process of actually transferring themselves to the alternative world than the majestic predestinarianism of Calvinism allowed.

Evangelicals feel deeply identified with the old American heritage of the pioneers and the soil. Yet as America has changed people of pioneer tradition have seen their status change. Power and population have shifted to the cities. The cities in turn have been filled with more recent immigrants of Roman Catholic, Eastern Orthodox, and Jewish faiths. The promise of the pioneer movement, the building of the Kingdom of God in the wilderness, ended with the creation of a new world in which a man of the old promise seemed a stranger. To such a person the evangelical faith holds out belief that the true aristocracy of the earth is not the mighty, but those who have accepted Christ, and that this status could be marked by abstinences which made the hard, isolated rural life morally triumphant.

Attitudes of the evangelical tradition toward American society may be summarized as follows:

1. The evangelicals feel nostalgic for an earlier America of the pioneers in which the faith of their spiritual forebears is idealized; this leads to a conservative affirmation of traditional American symbols and institutions.
2. There is also a reformism which usually centers around a few symbolic issues, such as opposition to the liquor trade or to foreign or Roman Catholic influences. These issues essentially pit evangelical life styles and moral values against strongly contrasting ones. Thus in the nineteenth century evangelicals lent support to the temperance and abolition of slavery causes and to the founding of colleges in the West where their value systems were taught.
3. Evangelicals in any given period will be opposed to a current educational, urban, and cultural "Establishment" from which they feel alienated: people who drink, do not believe the Bible literally, and are changing the country in directions contrary to evangelical values.
4. The individual experience emphasis leads to confrontational as well as withdrawal attitudes toward the "outside." Rhetoric stresses the drawing of lines between sides; forays such as urban missions and revivals are sent into the "other camp." The com-

bined sense of reformism and alienation, incidentally, has led to a difficult ambivalence toward education, especially higher education. Awareness that a word-centered faith ought to give priority to study is balanced by the fact that evangelicals have very often deprecated intellectualism and education, insofar as they conflict with the conversion experience and the gifts of the Spirit as the criteria of salvation or as the main qualification for preaching. Education which raised difficulties for the concept of full verbal inspiration of Scripture has been held especially dangerous.

5. This confrontational attitude necessitates an almost unavoidable mentality of an isolated, alienated, almost oppressed minority among the adherents of evangelicalism, even while they also feel they are the "real" Americans and that in some paradoxical sense the great "silent majority" of Americans are like them. In a way this is true; while serious evangelicals are a minority, probably most Protestant Americans have somewhere guilty feelings that if they were serious about religion, they would be like the evangelicals.

6. The activism and sense of isolation from the "outside" reinforce each other in the evangelical mentality. With a vigor like that of small town lodges and chambers of commerce, evangelical institutions work hard to promote rallies, Sunday schools, tours, programs, and revivals. Sporting and military terms, and often the heroes of these fields, are part of the vocabulary. Yet evangelicalism rarely lacks the feel of a belligerent but beleaguered army surrounded by its foes. It must be that this mentality is somehow necessary to the self-identity evangelicalism gives to its adherents. They are happiest as a minority assured that a revival is going on which may vindicate them in the near future. They love statistics indicating growth and often post them conspicuously in churches. This is activism induced by deferred reward thinking, in contrast to those more mystical religions stressing enjoying the present moment with God.

In sum evangelicalism in America has historically been a religion of persons who find themselves in a detached, alienated position within a changing or rejecting culture. Its short path personal experience orientation provides a way of integrating oneself and making meaningful, or interpreting, one's position in such a situation. It was so with the isolated pioneers on the frontier, in the defeated South after the Civil War, with the "old Americans" during the great waves of immigration and industrialization, and it is so with the epigoni of the 1960s youth culture who are now turning to the evangelical Christ.

THE STORY OF AMERICAN EVANGELICALISM

This history of evangelicalism in America has been intimately bound up with the history of revivals. The intense crowd fervor of those occasions, with their intertwined threads of nostalgia, miracle, and electric change, has brought vast numbers of people into the evangelical alternative world. While some more bookish evangelicals have disparaged the emotionalism of the revivals, by and large they have been the life of the movement. Revivals—great singing and preaching meetings held at places and by preachers independent of ordinary churches and aiming at personal decisions for Christ—have made evangelicalism something more than a denominational tradition. Included in revivalism also is the work of circuit riders, street evangelists, and skid row missioners, for these have, on a smaller scale, shared its methods and attitudes.

The revival preacher, with his folksy humor, his impassioned appeals, his lively or wistful songs, his healing touch and his power to open the gates of another world in a sawdust-strewn tent or bare barn, is the shaman and wandering minstrel of American pop religion. In his glowing unblinking eyes, which can seem to hold like forceps, his showmanship, his holding the Bible up like an ikon or a drum, there is the charisma of the medicine man and holy man of old. This charisma is very different from that of those whose religious position derives from education or ecclesiastical office—teachers and priests—however saintly.

The shaman-evangelist is a man of the people. He does not descend with priestly blessing, or smelling of the library, as from a higher sphere. He should have a background similar to that of the ordinary people to whom he speaks; he should use the same vocabulary, tell the same kind of jokes, talk about crops and money, or the street scene, in the same way they do, only better. If he has a college and seminary education, or even a doctor's degree, he conceals its effects as far as possible (though the mere use of the title Dr. is acceptable). He is, in other words, a charismatic holy man who has received his charisma in a way which leaves him within the circle of pop culture. He does not move away from the people into a literary or institutional "great tradition." He is anointed in a way which seems accessible to the man of pop culture, so that they can say, "Although he has tremendous belief and power, he's still one of us."

His nonhistorical way of speaking, making Scripture contemporaneous, using set words as symbols for states of consciousness derived from the alternative world, the appeal for decision rather than intellectual comprehension all mark him as "one of us"—one who has become holy and charismatic in a "folk" rather than in an institutional way. Therefore he can initiate others of the folk culture through the same doors. Pop culture religion is always fundamentally folk religion, cosmic and initiatory in orientation, not really taking seriously historical time, literary tradition, institutional structure, or the kind of charisma these rational traditions impart. The presence of the shaman is what counts—the man from among us who has gone to the other side, come back laden with its power, and who can show others the way—now, amid the flaring torches of a summer's night, during the slack season between seedtime and harvest.

Because evangelicalism has fitted into the folk religion pattern so well in America, through the work of the revivalist, the circuit rider, and the urban missionary, it has made those whose world is still fundamentally that of seasons and soil (and also the dispossessed of all sorts whose religious needs are for immediate experience of an alternative world) feel that evangelicalism is especially theirs. Liberal denominational churches, affected by the "social gospel" movement, may be deeply concerned about the lot of the urban and rural poor, but the poor themselves are most likely to turn to an evangelical or pentecostal church.

The strongest source of American evangelicalism is the Methodism of John Wesley, who preached the necessity of an experience of personal conversion and the "holiness" doctrine of possible perfection to the lower classes of eighteenth century England.

His movement was represented in America by such powerful preachers as George Whitefield. The nation's consciousness had been made fertile by the revival of the 1740s, the "Great Awakening" sparked in large part by the preaching of Jonathan Edwards, the Calvinist of Northampton, Massachusetts. Both Whitefield and Edwards began, in the evangelical pattern, by planting a conviction of sin. Edwards's image of "sinners in the hand of an angry God" held as by spider webs over the pit of hell is well known. Benjamin Franklin was impressed that Whitefield's audience "admir'd and respected him, not withstanding his ... assuring them they were naturally *half beasts and half devils.*"

It was on the frontier, however, that revivalistic evangelicalism as we know it was shaped. Here Calvinism was almost entirely forsaken for Wesleyan conversion with its intensity of experience. The frontiersman lived a hard and violent life; his turning to Christ was equally hard and violent—he took the kingdom of heaven by storm. Out of isolated cabins in a thousand lonely hollows in Kentucky, Ohio, and further west, from cabins to which hunger, sickness, and death were not strangers, from communities whose diversions often included little more than drunkenness and fighting, came spirit-hungry people as the word "revival" spread.

The initiating and archetypal event of frontier religion was the famous Cane Ridge revival of the first year of the nineteenth century. A lank Scotch-Irish Presbyterian with piercing eyes, the Reverend James McGready, had been licensed as a minister in 1788 at about thirty. Uncompromising against all he considered evil, he not surprisingly had a stormy career. He had to leave one congregation abruptly after receiving a warning written in blood.

In 1800 he was serving three small frontier churches in Logan county, Kentucky. After a sacramental service at one of these churches at which McGready and several other ministers spoke, a great fervor seized the congregation. Spiritually speaking, "the floor was covered with the slain; the screams for mercy pierced the heavens." Children of ten and twelve prayed in anguish for redemption. Later meetings under McGready continued to fill the forests with the groaning, shouting, preaching, sobbing frenzy of rough pioneer men, women, and children turning to the throne of grace.

The culmination of this series of meetings was the Cane Ridge revival beginning August 6, 1801. Multitudes came from as far away as a week's journey. They lived in tents and wagons in a vast circle around the meeting site. As many as 10,000 may have been present. Several preaching stands were set up. Ministers and laymen, whites and blacks, exhorted the milling, excited crowd incessantly. Refreshment stands did a rapid business; campfires blazed at night. Even pouring rain did not dampen the spiritual fervor.

Soon Cane Ridge was swept with signs of the Power. Converted pioneers broke uncontrollably into laughing, singing, shrieking (the "shout of victory"), falling down into cataleptic states, the "jerks," and dog-like barking ("treeing the devil"). Many who came only for amusement were unable to resist the persuasion of these phenomena; to their own great surprise they found themselves doing the same things as the others.

Why did pioneers pour into Cane Ridge? Today, their ordinary life would seem almost unbelieveably cramped, isolated, and deprived. The opportunity to visit friends, to mingle with crowds and hear music and sermons, to let out feelings long pent up, must have had great attraction. Mainly, however, they wanted to be given a true alternative world. They anticipated and desired a hard, intense, convincing experience of "being saved" or "being born again." They wanted to discover feelings, to have something really new and important happen in their private histories.

For all its seeming lonely isolation the frontier was a forge on which a new society was being wrought. Revivalism swept quickly across the frontier after Cane Ridge. The passions aroused by it led to new denominations—Cumberland Presbyterians, Disciples, Church of Christ—but it was the Methodists who managed to make the most of the situation. Their theology emphasizing individual decision and the possibility of perfection was precisely what the frontiersman could grasp. Since he had made the decision to leave the cramped seaboard lands for the wilderness, he could decide to set foot on this other trail as well. He was building a new world where there was a fresh chance for a human life without the evils of the old order. In this situation possibly even the grim judgment on human nature laid down by Calvin could be abrogated by grace working through such intense experiences as at Cane Ridge.

The Methodist circuit riders—preachers who rode from place to place along the frontier carrying the Good News—met the needs of the time. With little education, usually, but imbued with deep evangelical conviction and heroic dedication, they brought the gates of an alternative world to the farthest and humblest cabin. Their dogged perseverance bespoke a faith the pioneer could admire. (During a downpour, he would say, "Nobody out but ducks and Methodist preachers.") The circuit rider's spiritual world, in which you could speak to God as to a neighbor, where the Holy Ghost flew through the woods like a dove from meeting to meeting and miracles occurred weekly brought "otherness" to bone-hard lives.

Revivals, circuit riders, and conversion-oriented denominations planted evangelicalism firmly in the heartland and laid the groundwork for the future nostalgic association of evangelicalism with that epic period in American history. But during the frontier era itself, American society was in flux and formation. Evangelicalism, for all its seeming conservatism, was also an instrument for social change, often more effectively than denominations whose spokesmen talked more liberally. Wherever the psychic warmth of evangelicalism is found, change is going on. Its confrontational intensity is a forge upon which new patterns of personality—which can in turn affect society—are wrought. Its emphasis on individual experience makes it less amenable to structure in society; out of such democratic phenomena as Cane Ridge and circuit rider religion new social attitudes can emerge.

The evangelical convert may come away from the revival believing that the "old-time religion" is good enough, and nothing scholars or reformers say amounts to anything better. But he may also come away believing that anyone whose heart is right with God is as good as any other man, and that those who sit in the counting houses and society churches of the great cities are cold hypocrites whose day will come.

Thomas Jefferson was in the White House at the time of the Cane Ridge meeting. There could scarcely be a mind further removed from its experience than that of this liberal, cultured Deist, who commended only the ethical doctrines of Jesus and expected that by the end of his life Unitarianism would prevail in the nation because of its persuasive rationality. Yet Jefferson was a slave holder, however reluctantly. At Cane Ridge blacks and whites gathered together. The New England evangelist Henry Ward Beecher never lost an opportunity to castigate the wealthy Unitarians for exploiting the poor in their factories despite their lofty talk of ethical religion. Indeed, the first racially integrated churches in the South—as far back as 1910—were not in "liberal" denominations but were pentecostal.

Many religious movements swept through the spiritually restless first half of the nineteenth century in America. Besides evangelicalism and revivalism, there was transcendentalist idealism, Unitarian and Universalist rationalism, Spiritualist seances, Utopian communes of all sorts, and Swedenborgian mystics like John Chapman (Johnny Appleseed) who carried the idea of reverence for life and visits to heaven and hell to cabins in upper Ohio. All had in common at least the ideas that experience is the forge and test of spiritual reality, and that now, in the American *novus ordo seclorum* being wrought in the wilderness, perfection was a lively possibility.

After McGready, the next great revival preacher was another Presbyterian, Charles Finney. He began his work in 1824 in upstate New York. Finney was a tall man, craggy-faced with dark, deep-set eyes. He started in law, but as a young man experienced a tremendous baptism of the Holy Spirit, which changed his career. He describes it in these words:

> The Holy Spirit descended upon me in a manner that seemed to go through me, body and soul. I could feel the impression, like a wave of electricity, going through and through me. Indeed it seemed to come in waves of liquid love . . . It seemed like the very breath of God. I can recollect distinctly that it seemed to fan me, like immense wings . . .

Finney became in short order a master of denunciatory "hell fire" preaching designed to bring his listeners down to abject, writhing conviction of sin and turning to grace. He battered Unitarians and Universalists, and like most revivalists was a strong temperance man. He ended his career as an abolitionist and president of Oberlin College, which admitted blacks and women long before the Civil War, but he was always above all a preacher.

Evangelicalism and revivalism in the middle of the nineteenth century began to take new forms. With the passing of the old frontier, the generation reached by the circuit riders and meetings of the Cane Ridge sort also passed. A new brand of revivalists who had learned the craft, but who might lack the pristine fire, took the place of the old. They were professionals who knew how to use novelty, humor, and miracle in the context of a well-honed revival ideology of moving from feelings of depravity to ecstasy.

What reforming power there was in evangelicalism also passed. The Civil War made obsolete one of its two main social planks, the abolition of slavery, and temperance became increasingly an "old American" bulwark against the growing hordes of European immigrants, few of whom had any such attitude in their cultural background. New paths sprang up within the evangelical milieu, such as Seventh-Day Adventism, with its radical apocalyptic expectation of the imminent return of Christ.

Revivalism and evangelicalism retained plenty of life, however. The greatest revival preacher of all, Dwight L. Moody, was yet to appear. Moody (1837-99) dominated American evangelicalism in the post-Civil War era. Those were days of a busy, aggressive America, building railways, industrial empires, and vast fortunes. It was an America rapidly changing socially from the largely rural, Anglo-Saxon, and Protestant land of the frontier revivals to an urban, industrial society inhabited by a mixed multitude. New attitudes and ideas—social liberalism, Darwinism—were abroad. It was a time marked on the surface by confidence and self-satisfaction. The Horatio Alger myth of success by hard work was widely believed to mean everyone received the social standing he deserved.

Yet beneath the surface lay no small measure of sorrow, anguish, and uncertainty in the lives of countless individuals. Half of a family's children might very likely die at home before reaching maturity. Millions languished in hideous slums, racked by poverty, debt, and disease. Society had only the scantest provision for the indigent and the aged. Millions more hovered between success and failure, not sure whether the American dream was fulfilled for them or not. Multitudes were confused by the ongoing transition of America from a rural to an urban-industrial nation, half yearning for the old, unable to cope completely with new social and scientific ideas.

Into this world strode Dwight L. Moody, a Massachusetts farm boy who came to Chicago in the 1860s to sell shoes. Before long he was selling the Gospel instead. He started by organizing wildly successful Sunday schools for slum boys. Though not a minister, he was soon preaching too. Moody was a big man of over two hundred pounds, with driving energy and tireless determination to match that of any Carnegie or Vanderbilt, and a warm, compassionate, compelling personality.

The dynamic which animated this tremendous powerhouse was not desire to amass a fortune, but a call to preach Christ. His deep conviction was that accepting Christ was the one and only thing needful. He didn't have to waste much time portraying the guilt and terror of the unsaved, so well could his enthusiasm hold up the joy and peace of belief. His language was simple, sometimes ungrammatical, but rich in an imaginative contemporizing of the Bible, which Moody believed implicitly. Inseparable from Moody in his work was Ira B. Sankey, his song leader, master of evangelical hymns.

Moody's message, and that of Sankey's hymns even more, was full of simple assurance, of erring children found, of lost sheep discovered, of heaven as a home where all would be reunited and all tears wiped away. All this was the reward of accepting Christ and "becoming a Christian." Moody also developed the technique of revivals to a fine point. Advertising, seating arrangements of the "tabernacle," distribution of tickets, crowd control, small group meetings with the "saved"—all these were thoroughly organized and planned for in advance.

After Moody others without his greatness of heart imitated his techniques. Some evangelists and songsters, like Gypsy Smith, Charlie Alexander, and P. P. Bliss, were almost vaudeville in style. They showed once again the soul-winning success of deliberate breaks with pulpit style in favor of a folksy idiom with entertainment value. Others succumbed to the temptations of negativity, complementing appeals to rural nostalgia with acid attacks on rum, foreigners, and "modernism." The best known revivalist of that generation, Billy Sunday, organized his campaigns with the finesse of Moody, specifying also (which Moody did not) a sawdust hall and an advance financial guarantee. His music director, Homer Rodeheaver, was a master of the gospel trombone, who gave off the small-town heartiness of a Kiwanis Club toastmaster. Sunday brought a deliciously slangy diction to a vehement attack on liquor and the affectations of high society sinners, though he numbered among his friends many wealthy industrialists who thought his temperance message and economic conservatism good for the workingman.

PENTECOSTALISM

In the meantime, a new force of immense consequence for evangelicalism and the Jesus movement of today was breaking through. This was pentecostalism. Born with the new century, as revivalism was with the last, it had grown from struggling beginnings among the most dispossessed of American society, the blacks and "poor whites" of the rural South and the lowliest of the urban proletariat of both races, to become by the seventies a "third force" in Christianity. Undoubtedly the major contribution of America to world Christianity, pentecostalism is by far the fastest growing sizable form of that religion in much of the "third world." In South America and Africa pentecostalism will quite likely be the major form of active Christianity by the end of the century. In connection with this it is interesting to observe that some projections indicate that by the year 2000 Christians on those two continents will outnumber those on the other five. As a result of this mushrooming growth at home (including its manifestation in much of the Jesus movement) and abroad, pentecostalism has some 35 million adherents around the world.

Apart from its denominational strength, the 1960s saw a remarkable growth of pentecostal practice in the "mainline" denominations, including Roman Catholicism. Once again, evangelical Christianity—now in Pentecostal guise—has found ways to steal from traditionalism and revolutionary ideologies alike the allegiance of "the wretched of the earth," or more precisely the allegiance of those once wretched whose lives, while improving somewhat materially, are caught up in baffling change, uncertainty, and the emotional void of modernity. Or, it provides a vehicle for those surfeited with modernity who want instead the intensity of primal religious expression.

Pentecostalism has roots in the Wesleyan doctrine of Christian perfection as the result of the conversion experience. Many in this tradition held that after conversion you can receive a "second blessing" from the Holy Spirit which would preserve you in a sinless life. It was but a short step to believe that a community informed with this blessing should possess all the marks of the New Testament church and its spiritual signs and powers as well—healing, the power to pick up serpents, and above all the ability to speak in new tongues (glossalalia) as did the apostles on the day of Pentecost, when witnesses at first thought them full of new wine.

Phenomena similar to this—the barking and the "holy laugh"—were well known to the frontier revivals. After the Civil War an upsurge of enthusiasm for the "holiness" tenet, the belief that after "becoming a Christian" and receiving the Holy Spirit one can live a sinless life, occurred especially in the South. The National Holiness Alliance was founded in 1867. The remaining years of the century were taken up with controversy within the Southern Methodist fold over "holiness;" when "holiness" advocates finally felt no longer welcome, several new denominations appeared—Free Methodist, Nazarene, and others.

"Tongues" had been known among various medieval and reformation period sects as well as among the "Irvingites" of nineteenth century England. It was not until the beginning of the twentieth century, however, that these strands were brought together into a coherent structure: belief that speaking in tongues is a sure sign of full gospel conversion and a mark, therefore, of true and full Christianity.

The modern American movement began in 1901 in Topeka, Kansas, under the leadership of Charles Fox Parham. A Methodist of "holiness" conviction, Parham had begun a Bible school in Topeka in the fall of the previous year. He and his students had come to feel that something further was needed to evidence the gift of the sanctifying Spirit. After Bible study, they accepted that it was "speaking with other tongues." Then, at a watchnight service on December 31, 1900, a student of the school, Agnes N. Ozman, asked Parham to lay hands on her and pray for her to be baptized with the Holy Spirit. After midnight, on the first dawn of the new century, she allegedly began "speaking in the Chinese language." Tongues had come. Shortly after, the other students too found new languages. Much nationwide publicity accompanied these events.

The Jerusalem of the new tongues movement, despite its Kansas beginnings, was the great Azusa Street meeting in Los Angeles. A black preacher, William J. Seymour, had attended a class Parham conducted in Texas, and shortly after was called to preach in Los Angeles. In April of 1906, under his inspiration, a great revival began centering around speaking in tongues. It was contemporaneous with the San Francisco earthquake to the north, a fact not lost on those seeking confirmation of Seymour's prophecies of destruction. Beginning with blacks, the movement grew until whites were thronging to the meetings as well. The founders of several pentecostal denominations, both black and white, received initiation into the movement at Azusa Street. From this explosive beginning, the pentecostal churches expanded around the world.

Pentecostalism was not just evangelicalism with an additional fillip. As familiarity with the movement grows, it becomes increasingly evident that it is not, as it has sometimes been called, "ultra-fundamentalism" or extremist evangelicalism. It is instead a new way of experiencing Christianity, and one which demonstrates the continuing vitality of that religion.

In pentecostalism the alternative world is not merely *entered* through an experience of ecstatic commitment to it symbolized by Jesus. The same intensity *continues* to reinforce the experience of "two worlds" by continuing to break through regularly in the course of the Christian life. "Tongues" is a continuing miraculous confirmation of life on a transformed and alternative plane. In pentecostal churches speaking in tongues, together with their spiritual atmosphere, provides the believer with a tremendous sense of lightness and release. The pentecostalist has an experience of the active *reality* of the Holy Spirit, not just as a "still, small voice" but as an explosive power.

Gary Schwartz, in his comparative study of Seventh-Day Adventist and pentecostalist attitudes, portrays the difference in tone that the latter experience induces.[5] Adventist belief suggests a "harsh, demanding God" who expects precise observance of his commandments. But

> it promises success in this world and in the kingdom shortly to come to those who honor God's commands punctiliously. It equates the practical virtues which enhance one's chances for upward social mobility with the characteristics of God's elect, insuring that those who take God's stern warnings seriously will also strive to prove that they belong to this highly favored group.[6]

As pictured by Schwartz, Seventh-Day Adventism suggests that sort of activism inspired by the kind of deferred reward thinking we have described. It attracts people of those classes left behind by society by providing them with a compelling rationale for the kind of behavior that produces a sense of worth and upward mobility. At the same time the expectation of the imminent return of Christ and world judgment provides expectation of vindication and a sense of the closeness of the alternative world.

But Schwartz points out that the pentecostal image of God is different. He is benign and can accomplish great transformations now. "Anything is possible for those who open their hearts to Jesus and accept whatever provisions God makes for them."[7] Even *now* a person can attain salvation and supernatural powers. For the pentecostalists, the successes and failures of this life have no abiding meaning; they are nothing compared to the joys of the other world that they freely experience.

Thus the pentecostalist is likely to be far less concerned than the Adventist about occupation and status. He is more definitely detached from the systems and values of the world and more radically identified with another. Schwartz found that the pentecostalist is likely to have a lower socioeconomic standing and less stability in family life.

His church structure is also likely to be more fluid. The pentecostalist minister may be less well educated, in a conventional sense, than most ministers of any other denomination. He may utter "queer" prophecies and move erratically from one city to another. Women, like the well-known Aimee Semple McPherson, may serve as prominant evangelists and ministers. The ordination of women is certainly not an "ultra-fundamentalist" characteristic, though pentecostalists justify it by the Bible verse, "Your daughters shall prophesy."

The history of doctrinal controversy within the pentecostal movement indicates that conventional orthodoxy was not taken for granted. In 1916, for example, the Assemblies of God church was split between trinitarians and those who held to the "oneness" doctrine that baptism should be in the name of Jesus only, who in himself embraced the fullness of God. But the radicality of such unusual beliefs as that only Jesus is God, now held by the "Pentecostal Assemblies" family of churches, may be overlooked due to the fact they do not follow the patterns of ordinary liberalism either. While such teaching may be founded on "searching the Scriptures," the pentecostalist divine does not seem to read them deductively or analytically. He leaps into it with a Spirit-inspired eclecticism and ability to free associate into strikingly unusual intuitive patterns of meaning the most unlikely verses, moods, and current situations. He moves agilely from luminous verse to subjective feeling to contemporary application, unbound by much dogmatic superimposition.

This pentecostal fire could not be contained within the denominational structures of the first generation of pentecostalists. About 1960 a speaking in tongues movement began within the mainline denominations. To their surprise students, seminarians, clergy, and laity in the Episcopal, Presbyterian, and other supposedly staid Protestant denominations found themselves praying or praising God in words other than English, usually a wholly "unknown" language whose meaning they could only surmise.[8]

One Episcopal clergyman of my acquaintance says that tongues came to him while he was seeking, in great anguish of spirit, for words when praying with a desparately ill parishioner. With the "tongues" came a powerful upsurge of spiritual energy which transformed the situation for both. Since then this minister has found that the same gift of tongues appears in his personal devotions. He leads an interdenominational weekly prayer group in which both "gospel singing" and the tongues phenomena occur. Located in a small northern city to which a number of southerners, both blacks and whites, have migrated, this group attracts persons of all races, of both traditionally pentecostal and "mainline Protestant" backgrounds. It is doubtless typical of the quiet but persistent way in which the pentecostal experience has been permeating Christian life of America.

On another occasion, I heard a minister of a major church definitely in the New Thought tradition describe receiving the gift of tongues. He was participating in a service of healing sponsored by a nondenominational pentecostal layman's organization. Ten ministers in the front of the church prayed for the baptism of the Holy Spirit. It came, he said, as laughter, the laughter of God. They didn't even recognize it as the

Holy Spirit at first, but simply accepted the gales of deep, rich, and utterly joyous laughter which arose out of them as a deep release of ecstasy. It was not shrill or hysterical but profound and divine. Everyone just laughed for about ten minutes; during this time one lady with arthritis was healed. She was still laughing as she left.

Local and nationwide pentecostal organizations now exist within virtually all denominations. Recently, and with tremendous power, the pentecostal movement has swept through the Roman Catholic church. "Tongues" groups have appeared at Notre Dame and many other Catholic campuses.

Naturally a movement as dramatic as this was bound to be controversial. Some clergymen lost their jobs because of opposition to their "tongues" activity. The Rev. Dennis Bennett, former rector of a large Episcopal church in the Van Nuys section of Los Angeles, offered his resignation in 1960 after his experience of "tongues" and his work with a group in the church which practiced it caused dissension. "Tongues" have often created division. Non-tongues-speakers are frequently unable to accept the existence of the practice in their churches. They resent the implication that their own spiritual lives are lacking and feel that the "tongues" groups are cliquish and flaunt their newfound "gift" as if it were a mark of special sanctity. Many tongues-speakers, to be sure, in their enthusiasm have not always been tactful.

The pentecostal movement outside the pentecostal churches is characteristically marked by a quiet, devotional style rather than by shouting and excited moving about. Meetings are held in living rooms more often than in churches. The attenders, seated comfortably, will sing hymns, listen to Bible reading, discuss the passage, and then pray quietly and sponteneously. The feeling is, "We will now speak softly with God; if you feel like speaking in tongues, that is all right; if not, that is all right too." But many strange sounds, soft and fast, often repeated, may be heard. The leader may lay hands on persons desiring to receive the Holy Spirit for blessing and "tongues." Usually the group is also deeply concerned with healing and will direct prayer and perhaps laying on of hands to this end too. Those who speak in "tongues" generally believe quite explicitly in the power of prayer; their prayers are specific and confident.

All these ramifications of American evangelicalism—conversion, biblicism, holiness, and pentecostalism both within and without the older pentecostal churches—have come together in the Jesus movement. In the Jesus movement, evangelicalism is playing a familiar role: providing a set of experiences and a rhetoric which give expression to a group increasingly self-isolated from the cultural mainstream and legitimitizes their sense of having had a separate experience from both cosmic and social points of view. In the Jesus movement, it plays for the youth culture the same role it has played before in the identity-quest of frontiersmen, southerners after the defeat in the Civil War, blacks, and skid row down-and-outers.

Nonetheless, there is a new flavor in the Jesus movement related to the new youth culture out of which many of its participants have come, for theirs is a new kind of isolation, caused not by geography, defeat, racial prejudice, or poverty, but by the creation of a novel middle-class generational culture cleavage. It is striking that for some this family-based crisis should have the historical dimensions of the frontier or the Civil War, and call up a traditional religious response of proportionate scale, but such is the case. We will now look at the phenomena of the Jesus movement itself.

3

The Jesus Experience

THE JESUS MOVEMENT AS RELIGIOUS EXPERIENCE

THE LATE TEENS AND EARLY TWENTIES seem to be the golden age of religious experience. Later in life, religious experience may be repeated, reinforced, or even (in the case of those who cannot be brought to it save out of many vicissitudes) acquired. C. G. Jung, in fact, considered the second half of life the religious half. He argued that it is only then that the individual sets out on his true, mature quest for integration of the fragments of his psyche and for a basis of life beyond the biological. The first half of life, Jung said, is sexual in the psychoanalytic sense; even its sometimes explosive religious passions are fired as much by libido as by spirit.

That may be so. The mature silver age of faith may be richer, more balanced, or more desperate than that of youth. It may be a faith wrought out of torments unknown to youth, or out of a wisdom found when all the idols of the library and the marketplace have crumbled. Or, it may be the wistful formulae of an aged votary seeking to recover what he felt at twenty-two.

But mature faith rarely has the pristine glow, the fiery absoluteness, or the life-forming totality of the adolescent conversion. It is then that people see what it seems has never been seen before, feel raptures they believe have never been so deeply felt—certainly not in their families—and leave all to join monasteries or to seek the feet of a guru.

The golden age experience has taken many forms. At various times in recent history young people have flocked to become Trappist monks and Zen meditators. Now thousands are finding a new-old vehicle of expression for it—evangelical Christianity. As we have seen, evangelicalism is not new to America. Nor is it new as an enthusiasm of the young. Its preachers have brought countless youth before to the yoke of Christ, and its missions and Bible colleges have not lacked recruits. But what is new, at least in our century, is the joining of this old tradition with the avant-garde, cutting edge of the culture of youth drifting, searching, half-alienated from their presumptive roots. The devout Bible college youth of yesterday, in the days between the great revivals and the Jesus movement, carried with his big black Bible a clean-shaven, dark-suited, pious image. People sensed he had been a star Sunday school pupil and that he came from an evangelical family which neither drank nor smoked. Today's leader of the Jesus movement holds the same Bible, but he is more likely to sport electric long hair and rather unconventional clothes. More to the point, instead of coming from a devout, conservative home, he will as likely as not have passed through drugs and perhaps more than one wildly erratic life style on his way to the cross.

Both of these evangelists, however, are seeking to share a particular religious experience with others. It is a fundamental premise of this book that the Jesus movement is basically a *religious* movement and that religion plays a unique role in human life. Religious movements, attitudes, symbols, and meanings, in my view, represent a distinct configuration of experiences in man, and cannot be merely reduced to psychological, sociological, or historical explanations, though analysis of these and other factors all assist greatly in understanding them.

But what seems to be the implicit goal of religious experience and rite is transformation of self and world into a different, unconditioned, ultimate state in harmony with the hidden absolute nature of reality. Religious man senses that the unexamined personality, torn by its varying desires, pleasures, and frustrations, threatened by extinction, is of little worth unless his inner life can somehow be transformed into a process unlimited by these conditions. Something deep in his consciousness tells him that man has a potential for this transformation. Yet it seems the gate is narrow and the key lost. The world's panorama of religious practice, rite, and technique, from Buddhist meditation to evangelical conversion, is intended to give subjective assurance that the transformation has taken place, or is taking place, thus liberating the self to become whole and integrated.

In the same way religious man senses that the life of the ordinary workaday world is not enough to make human existence seem worthwhile without those moments of really intense joy when he lives on a different plane. Such moments come to individuals in various ways and times. Religion strives to create them, as part of its process of ultimate transformation, through festival, rite, music, and drama.

The definition of religion used is by Frederick Streng—"means of ultimate transformation."[9] The state of ultimate transformation itself is not religion; rather, religion is the *means* toward it, and whatever appears in human life as a means toward ultimate transformation is religion.

Means of ultimate transformation may be analyzed in terms of the three forms of religious expression presented by the sociologist of religion Joachim Wach.[10] These are: theoretical, or what is thought and said —narrative, myth, doctrine, philosophy; practical, or what is done— rite, worship, behavior; and social—the kind of interpersonal relationships and group structures formed. A religious movement is a shared quest for ultimate transformation centering around particular embodiments and constellations of these forms of expression. The quest for means of ultimate transformation always seems to create expression in all three of these forms. If all three are not present, it may be questioned whether a particular phenomenon is really "religion" in the sense of a working means toward ultimate transformation.

If a movement is not actually "ultimate" but is merely reformist and oriented toward finite goals, it is not "religious." Nor is it "religious" if it is just philosophic or moral speculation, rather than actually a "means," that is, a process actually functioning in the lives of individuals and society and aimed at the goal of the unconditioned state.

Theoretical expression without the other two forms is likely to be philosophy rather than religion. Practical expression without the other two may be private magic. Social expression without the other two could be a club. The quest for means of ultimate transformation, then, when answered by finding what the person accepts as a viable means, evokes an ultimate, unconditioned response. This means that none of the significant areas of human life—thought, word, action, symbol making, group formation—can be left untouched by the commitment.

It is not surprising, then, that the Jesus movement immediately manifested all three of these forms of expression—distinctive terminology, validating narratives, signs and modes of worship, and groups. For this reason, the Jesus movement can only be properly understood as a *reli-*

gious movement, with its roots in the eternal human quest for means of ultimate transformation. It images a life functionally integrating the three forms of expression to provide a combined experience which is a means toward ultimate transformation. None alone are the means—not the doctrine, nor the worship scenarios, nor the group life. All three together are necessary to put the suppliant in a state of subjective consciousness in which assurance of the powers of transformation working in him can be realized. The story the Jesus movement, like any other religious movement, tells us this. Together, the three forms create virtually an alternative reality, another world into which the believer can step, and where the finitude of this world is reversed.

THE CENTRAL RELIGIOUS MOTIF OF THE JESUS MOVEMENT

The next question is, Why has the Jesus movement acquired the particular forms that it has, as a religious movement? Let us look again at the cultural background of the movement. One way to understand particular religious expressions is to understand precisely what picture each gives of the unsatisfactory human situation. The nature of the means of transformation is conditioned in large part by the image of the situation a group would change. Paul Ricoeur, in *The Symbolism of Evil,* has described several ways in which man has pictured the involvement in guilt and evil which expresses his problem.[11] Some myths and religions use the language of defilement, impurity, and stain to describe the "feel" of unregenerate life in this world. Others talk of human rebellion such as that of Milton's Satan. Still others see man mainly as lost and strayed, an exile from his true home. Some have even pictured the gods themselves as capricious tricksters or as wicked beings from whom man can expect little friendship—and from whom he must save himself.

The basic symbol of evil for the Jesus movement seems to be *multiplicity.* The unconverted life is described as confused by countless options, symbols, and alluring paths. It is the world of innumerable beckoning experiences, too many for any one person to taste, except perhaps by living for a new one every day—drugs, easy sex, political involvement, overadvertised possessions and products. The world offers ways out of any problems these experiences may create, but only through other confusing pluralisms—any number of schools and techniques of occultism, meditation, enlightenment, and behind them a cosmos animated by a kaleidescope of Buddhas, Hindu gods, spirits of good and evil.

Merely living life day by day indicates choice after choice between responsibilities and opportunities—between parents and peers, home and freedom, levels of education, vocational options, styles of dress and manner of life, participation or not in the military. Probably no generation has ever had so much real freedom, in the sense of actual, clearly available possibilities held out—by friends, by television, in schools and the marketplace—ready to be grasped and held, at least for a moment, or passed by for something else. But how do you know how to know what you want, or what you should want for any reason? Or is it all a "miracle mystery play" behind which someone, or something, is laughing and mocking?

The Jesus movement's clear, direct answer to all this is the slogan "One Way!" One shining alternative in the midst of all the confusing phantasmagoria stands out—Jesus. The sign of the finger beside the cross pointing upward is repeated over and over on bumper stickers, posters, books, and in the context of worship. While guitar music twangs out old and new hymns, young devotees in levi jackets raise the solitary finger to heaven. They are expressing subjective assurance that the means of ultimate transformation is available *here,* and that the transformation is taking place in them *now.*

A religious movement acquires a life of its own. Yet it cannot help but draw motifs from the culture against which it is reacting, or accept the problem as stated by that culture. Thus the Jesus movement is a movement in interaction with the modern world of multiplicity. This world has been well portrayed by John B. Orr and F. Patrick Nichelson in their book, *The Radical Suburb.*[12] More a state of mind than a geographical place, the radical suburb is the world inhabited and made by the more creative of middle-income families—the background out of which a large proportion of Jesus people come, as did the "hippies" before them. Their new middle-class culture is "radical" in an unconscious life style sense rather than in a political sense. Its values are changing so that life is seen as a series of experiences rather than a single commitment shaped by tradition.

"Having a good experience" is the radical suburb's touchstone. Against the backdrop of a world shaped by rational, scientific institutions and tract homes at the end of freeways, radical suburb man tries to create for himself a series of fantasy experiences—home decorations, restaurants, and Disneyland worlds from all sorts of times and places. On television he watches the world as a series of ten-minute vignettes, where he can always change channels. His family, job, sports, and church life are series of roles he moves in and out of.

For many these serial experiences are more or less satisfactory. Insofar as radical suburb man has created what is, as the pattern of a whole society, a quite new way of being in the world for man, he is far more radical, and far more successful, than the political "radicals" locked into ideologies and single commitments as surely as the religious fanatics of the past. But there is one experience his serial experiences preclude—intensity. He is starved for intensity.

Intensity, or at least the sights and sounds of intensity, is of course offered in the multiplicity marketplace of modern society. The new sensuality in design, dress, entertainment, sexual frankness, and music offers it through embellishing the serial experiences, one by one, with richer color, louder noise, greater feeling, and more engrossing fascination than ever before. Political causes of left and right present vehicles for intense commitment, whether long- or short-term. But there is a price, as there is for everything.

The real cost is not in time or money, with which radical suburb man is sufficiently supplied. It is a sacrifice of a basic assumption of his society, that any good experience is good, not just that some are good. It is also costly in terms of his fundamental virtue, sincerity. Sincerity does *not* mean dogged commitment, but the converse—remaining with an experience only as long as you are *really* experiencing it. If you remain longer, you fall into playing a role, necessary perhaps in business, but recognized as gamesmanship and so regarded as not sincere or even respectable in avocational matters such as politics, aesthetics, or religion. Hence, save in those channels of experience that can deliver their ultimate intensity without preliminary dry preparation, the quest for intensity runs diametrically counter to the virtue of sincerity. For to be sincere in the modern sense is actually to be "cool," not to let yourself get too involved in anything emotionally—to be nonintense.

How can an activity be both "sincere" and "nonintense"? The model, once again, is television. To experience is to be spiritually passive, an observer or a participant-observer, a consumer. If you become intense, you have moved onto the stage, or rather into the TV studio, as an actor. This destroys the fantasy. Yet at the same time intensity, as the drama which draws the observers, is nonetheless the hidden pivot around which the dance moves, the taboo god, whom all worship in their rites of imitation but none dare touch.

The Jesus movement draws from this milieu. It speaks the language of life-as-experience and of experience-as-a-good-thing. It offers Jesus as the ultimate experience and as a means of transformation beyond the world. With its nostalgic overtones and its ersatz frontier simplicity, it is not lacking in elements of fantasy life. However, because its adherents have not known serial experience to be good, but instead to be terrifying and demonic, it counters with an experience which *is* absolute and so regarded as ultimately intense. The leaders—conveyors—

of the Jesus experience seem to validate their appeal chiefly because they communicate total sincerity in the traditional and modern sense simultaneously. They are "cool" in the sense that there is no hint they will go on to other experiences in the future; they are intense in that they radiate a fiery, total commitment.

THE JESUS MOVEMENT AND THE FORMS OF RELIGIOUS EXPRESSION

We will now turn to the analysis of the Jesus movement in terms of its structure and forms of expression. In speaking of it as a movement, we indicate that it is a social event which shares a common motif, but which exists in many forms and on many levels.

The movement is first of all a "cultural drift"—a widespread pattern of diffuse need and response expressed by distinguishable symbols, such as popular songs and media-disseminated awareness. Within the drift are "carrying organizations," small active groups and institutions—Jesus coffeehouses, street groups, periodicals, movement-centered churches.

To speak of drift and carrying organizations does not imply that, at least in this case, the movement arose spontaneously over a broad spectrum of population. Rather, the movement spread out in both "diffuse" and "active" ways from seeds planted by the evangelical and pentecostal traditions in the multiplicity and experience-wracked youth culture. The seeds were planted in several places and according to no calculated plan, but nonetheless it is significant to note that social movements like this have antecedents.

Both drift and carrying organization expressions seem to be acquiring more institutionalization as the movement's history progresses. Some groups are losing fluidity and becoming highly structured sects in their own right. For far more Jesus people, the movement is being assimilated into the church tradition in America. Patterns developed within the independent Jesus movement are being adopted by evangelical churches, thus obviating the need for a separatism. Sharing in the broader frontier, southern, and urban lineages of alienation, they are thereby integrating the new youth culture's species of alienation into that greater and older American heritage of what might be called "established alienation."

The Jesus movement itself is definable just as a movement, not as an institution or as any other organized system. It can therefore best be approached in terms of common characteristics, each of which relates to one of the Wachian forms of religious expression. Where a high percentage, though not necessarily all, of these characteristics obtain, a social phenomenon could be regarded as part of the Jesus movement.

1. *Theoretical expression.* Jesus movement doctrine centers around the "One Way" motif—Jesus is the sole saviour, the only doorway to heaven for the world. The apocalyptic theme that Jesus is coming soon and that we are entering a "time of troubles" before the end, is also central. Both are clearly ultimate transformation motifs. Conversion narratives, as validating stories, play an important role. The rhetorical style is usually affective, centering on feelings; uses contemporary "hip" language; and reflects a nonrational intensity. You do not communicate so much by reasoned argument as by revealing the strength of your own experienced conviction. Language expressing the joy of your commitment to Jesus tends to be very similar everywhere in the movement, especially within single groups, suggesting identification with an archetypal transformation experience and a desire not to deviate greatly from a group norm.

2. *Worship.* Practical or worship expression emphasizes the communication of symbols of intensity and religion as essentially a sensual experience. In both these respects music is the central vehicle and after it rhetoric. The musical and rhetorical idiom are contemporary, though fraught with overtones of nostalgia. Worship and evangelistic experiences offer freedom of individual expression in prayer, testimony, and speaking in tongues, but the language generally follows established models.

3. *Social expression.* Most Jesus people are between the ages of fourteen and twenty-four. Their backgrounds usually include some exposure to the "youth culture," including drugs. Like the "hip" society, they are generally of middle- or upper-middle-class white background. Again like the "hip" world, as many as 30 percent may be of Jewish background, indicating religious heritage is of less importance as a determinative of acceptance or rejection of Jesus movement conversion than being a part of a presently alienated subgroup. Perhaps, indeed, the long special Jewish history of insecurity within larger societies has contributed to the prominence, out of proportion to their numbers in the total population, of Jews in the "hip" and Jesus subcultures. The "Jews for Jesus" movement is allied to the Jesus movement, and the biblicism of the latter movement has produced a fascination with Judaism, Israel, and the chosen people idea that makes much of Jewish adherents, called not "converted" but "completed" Jews. Some wear a badge bearing a cross superimposed on a Star of David. The phenomenon is a part of the Jesus movement's new discovery of Christianity as the bearer of middle-class, alienated, detached sensitivity rather than of "establishment" values; Jews have known this life style a long time.

Organization in the Jesus movement is fluid, centering upon Bible classes, movement-related church services, and communal living. But there is also a great emphasis upon charismatic leaders, often somewhat older men who adopt the style and language of the younger people.

The Jesus movement can be compared to other phenomena in the history of religions, from early Christian monasticism to tantric and bhaktic Hinduism. It shares with early Christian monasticism a young and intense group rejecting the "world" of sensuality and multiplicity in favor of Christian communal devotion. It shares with tantrism the short path motif, and with bhakti belief that fervent devotion with songs, pledges, and service to a personal deity can bring the ultimate transformation of saving union with him. But like all religion in the concrete, it is also unique and cannot be explained just in terms of some other model or precedent.

THE STORY OF THE MOVEMENT

Everyone in the Jesus movement tells a different story about who started it and how. Here are some of the things that happened, some seeds that were planted. They are a sampling of concrete ways in which the One Way offering of ultimate transformation broke through in the youth culture of the late sixties.

In 1968, as the "hippie" movement was beginning to decline, a coffeehouse called The Living Room opened in the Haight-Ashbury district of San Francisco. There was a difference between it and the many other gathering places of the counter culture—the operators were evangelical ministers. It was not the first time a Christian coffeehouse had been established in the midst of alien territory. In the days of the Beatniks a decade before, a Congregational minister ran one called Bread and Wine. But The Living Room was different and bespoke a different religious situation. It was not oriented toward intellectual Christian existentialism, but toward a heavily biblical message.

Then in 1967 the Salt Company Coffee House opened in Hollywood under the auspices of the Hollywood Presbyterian Church. This church, the largest of the United Presbyterian denomination and traditionally evangelical in orientation, has had a marked impact on the evolution of the movement, largely due to the work of its Minister for College Work, the Rev. Don Williams. The decor and music typical of The Salt Company is country-western rather than psychedelic and rock. Evenings at the coffeehouse present music with a Jesus slant combined with scripture and an evangelical appeal to listeners to declare their love for Christ made by a young, mod-dressed entertainer.

Since its founding, thousands of young people have passed through the doors of the Salt Company from nearby Hollywood High School, from other churches, from the streets. The Salt Company has its own combo, which has played across the nation, and a shop selling Christian books and jewelry. In 1969, under its leadership, several thousand young people marched down Hollywood Boulevard in a Christian demonstration, on the heels of various demonstrations of other sorts. Again in 1970, on Easter morning another group marched to City Hall to tell the city of the Resurrection.

The coffeehouse, with its casual, vaguely conspiratorial yet easily controllable atmosphere is understandably popular both with young people and with adult workers trying to reach young people. It has had a key role in the Jesus movement in linking major churches and evangelical organizations with the street.[13]

Others, however, have not had the time or means for that kind of work; they have taken their message directly to the streets. From Long Beach came two evangelists named Harvey and Bob. They had a truck with speakers and megaphones. They had worked for some time on the waterfront as evangelists among longshoremen and drunks; about 1967 they began to spread their message in the habitats of the youth culture. Somehow, for many who had lost to drugs and the rhetoric of radical politics all the subtleties of refined discourse, what they said and the way they said it got through. Some of the strong people of the movement were originally converted by Harvey and Bob.

Their message, proclaimed through megaphones to streetcorner audiences, was very judgment-oriented. Repent, change your life, accept Christ, or God will damn you to eternal fire. Don Williams says the love of God can only be presented in a loving way, and he certainly personifies a caring, accepting, nonaccusatory approach. But some street people seem to respond only when told God Himself will hate them forever unless they change. They can respect most those evangelists with the boldness to shout this to them at the curbside. Simplicity attracts their attention, and talk of God's hatred amplifies the latent self-hatred related to their present life. The willingness of the street evangelist to undergo the ridicule of the "world" as a fanatic convinces them he is also alienated, like them, and speaks as one outcast to another. It shows he is not trying to make a name or career out of "helping" them, and thus is "sincere." The same bond which had long existed between the evangelist and the skid row drunk was growing up between him and the youthful drug derelicts and runaways.

Judgment is certainly the message of one of the "hardest" and most effective of the Jesus movement evangelistic teams, Tony and Sue Alamo. Formerly a Jewish record promoter, Tony Alamo was converted to Christ, and in 1967 he and his wife began a fundamentalist ministry to the street people. Moving several times from one location to another, often under pressure from neighbors who objected to the noisy services and scruffy clientele, the work has now centered on a ranch near Saugus, California, called the Christian Foundation. Meetings oriented toward Gospel music, decision for Christ in the face of God's impending judgment of all sinners, and the power of the Holy Spirit are held nightly and twice on Sundays.

A number of young people live a communal life under the close supervision of the Alamos on several farms around the Foundation. A bus is sent daily to Hollywood Boulevard. Members of the Foundation, generally in worn clothes and long hair, hand out slips of paper to passers-by stating REPENT OF YOUR SINS JESUS IS COMING SOON and offering a free ride in the bus to the evening service. As in the old-fashioned skid row missions, attenders will also get a meal. If a discussion occurs with one of these witnesses, the hearer will learn that God does not forgive lightly and that he had better repent now and believe all the Bible. The tone may be harsh and polemical.

An uncompromising tone has also been characteristic of much of the popular writing of the movement. If the coffeehouse has been its right arm, the throwaway newspaper has been its left. None is better known than Duane Pederson's *Hollywood Free Paper*.[14] After several years as a night club entertainer and after a stormy student career at an Assemblies of God college, Duane, then about thirty, came to California. Although his Jesus People House conducts Bible classes, sells Jesus posters and the like, Duane's major work has been the paper. It started in 1969 and now circulates in a number of cities. Issues have run up to a million copies, financed by subscriptions and donations, and the paper is given away on the streets. The *Hollywood Free Paper* offered directories of movement coffeehouses, "Jesus raps," and so forth, as well as accounts of converts from drugs and "the occult" to Jesus. It was full of cartoons in which spiritual emptiness may be represented by a character with a hole in his abdomen, and the "Bread of Life," conceptualized as a loaf of ordinary sliced white bread descending from above. Duane admits it was rather gross—he is a very likeable and not unsophisticated person—but argues that only the most pointed, black-and-white language could penetrate to the people he is trying to reach. A long-time heavy drug user has a very short attention span and can only respond to a decision situation put in terms of the most extreme alternatives. In 1972, as the movement natured, the tone of the paper grew more sophisticated.

But the first of the Jesus newspapers seems to have been *Right On!*, started in Berkeley by the World Christian Liberation Front on July 1,

1969, the same year as the *Hollywood Free Paper.* It is still the most literate and one which does not hesitate to discuss social and political issues from an evangelical perspective. In *Right On!* that perspective is not automatically identified either with political conservatism or radicalism.

Linda Meissner in Seattle started *Agapé* (the New Testament Greek word for "charity" or "love") a few days after the founding of *Right On!* Ms. Meissner has been one of the most effective organizers in the movement. Previously a missionary overseas and then a worker with the New York Assemblies of God minister Dave Wilkerson,[15] who has now disavowed connection with her work, she came to Seattle in the late sixties.

In Seattle Ms. Meissner organized a coffeehouse, The Catacombs, which received 2,000 young people a week. She also instituted Jesus People parades and Christian invasions of rock concerts, always with a flair for the dramatic gesture—in 1970 she rented a small plane and dropped 10,000 copies of *Agapé* from above on such a concert. When she joined the Children of God in 1971, the rest of the Jesus movement suffered a setback.

The Northwest has, by the way, been a center for the Jesus movement, just as it largely has been a West Coast phenomenon in its "cultural" forms. One reason was the work of Linda Meissner. Another has been the influence of Father Bennett's neopentecostalism in conventional churches, now centered in Seattle.

But the backgrounds of the founders of two other papers in the Northwest indicate the diversity of the movement's roots. *Truth* in Spokane was started by Carl Parks, a thirty-three year-old business executive who, in response to a deepening Christian commitment, and inspired by the sight of Linda Meissner's "Jesus People Army" march in Seattle at Easter, quit his job in 1970 to devote himself to work for Christ. *Maranatha* in Vancouver, British Columbia, was begun in 1970 by Jacob Grin, who met Christ in the midst of an LSD trip in 1968.

And with an even more diverse background, across the country, the New York Bible Society, a traditionally conservative group, began a street-idiom paper aimed at the Jesus people and prospective Jesus people called *Great News.*

Besides coffeehouses and papers, the Jesus movement has expressed itself through other forms: movement-related churches, like Calvary Chapel; extra-ecclesiastical organizations like Campus Crusade, Teen Challenge, and communes. A center called Way Out on the top two floors of the Ulfat Hotel in Kabul, Afghanistan, gives free snacks and Gospel to the many young wanderers, drug addicts, and spiritual questers who travel through central Asia in the summer. Arthur Blessit's His

Place was a Christian center specializing in ministering to runaways on the Sunset Strip; its founder won headlines by chaining himself to a large wooden cross on the Strip until he was able to overcome the opposition of local landlords and rent a building for a Jesus center in the middle of that nightclub and counter culture district.

SYMBOLS AND MUSIC OF THE MOVEMENT

Arthur Blessitt, when he was working on the Sunset Strip, used the well-known peace symbol topped by a cross to indicate that true peace is found only through Christ. I happened to be at His Place one evening when a small delegation from a suburban-based ultraconservative evangelical group arrived to protest the use of this sign, which they connected with everything evil from Communism to witchcraft. An assistant minister and I (as a historian of religion) tried to explain to them that all symbols have changing roles and essentially mean what they mean to the people who are using them.

The most popular symbol in the movement, however, is the image of a hand with the index finger pointed upward, and beneath it the words "One Way!" A small cross is placed beside the finger. It is the Jesus people's answer to the clenched fist of the activists and the two fingers of the peace sign. The symbol was designed by Lance Bowen, who managed the Salt Company Coffeehouse for its first year and a half. Later Bowen and his wife went to Hawaii, where they helped a group of Jesus people rebuild an abandoned missionary church. He reports that many of these people had previously been involved in witchcraft, drug, and occult groups dwelling in the Hawaiian back country, and he relates some hair-raising stories of conflict between black magic and the power of Christ. It is against this background that the effect of the "One Way" motif is evident. After soul-shaking but confusing experiences with all sorts of oriental gods, psychedelic visions, the faces on the Tarot cards, the powers contacted with witchcraft and magic, the attraction of a single path, of one sure and strong helping hand leading out of that psychic vortex becomes tremendously attractive.

The movement has also generated a rash of more dubious symbolic expressions, from the obligatory T-shirts and bumper stickers with slogans of the movement ("I'm a Jesus people"; "Fight truth decay: Read the Bible"; "In case of rapture this vehicle will self-destruct") to such commercial exploitation as Jesus wristwatches and roach clips.

But the great vehicle of the Jesus movement is music. The ability of Jesus rock and gospel melodies to generate rich, powerful feelings in a mood and emotion-oriented age has brought and held the movement together. It is largely music that has made the movement a part of pop culture, and it is the Jesus movement as pop culture that distinguishes it from what is going on in the churches.

In 1969 a San Francisco disc jockey played a vigorous shout-of-praise song called "O Happy Day." It quickly moved to number one on top-40 stations. Sung by a black group called The Edwin Hawkins Singers, this first musical success may have had as much to do with creating the movement as the other way around. Moreover, it established once again the key role of blacks (inspired ultimately by the black churches) in constructing American pop culture.

"O Happy Day" was soon followed in late 1970 by ex-Beatle George Harrison's "My Sweet Lord," and then by the phenomenal rock opera, "Jesus Christ, Superstar." It put the winsome figure of Jesus as a young hero at the center of pop awareness. "Superstar," however, is much criticized by hard-core Jesus people on the grounds that it distorts the New Testament, leaves out the resurrection (although it could be argued that it is simply based on the traditional passion oratorio model, like Bach's "St. Matthew Passion," which being designed for Holy Week use also ends with the death of Jesus), and makes Jesus too "human," too full of doubt and despair.

The Jesus movement has won a number of big name entertainers who support it, including Tiny Tim, Paul Stookey, Arlo Guthrie, and Johnny Cash. It has produced a plethora of singing groups and individuals mainly devoted to the Jesus message. One individual is Pat Boone, a long-time public Christian, but he is perhaps in a different category since his style is more traditional. However, Mr. Boone has recently tried hard to identify with the movement—he has experienced pentecostalism and has made his swimming pool available for movement baptisms.

Some of the best known Jesus singers are Larry Norman, Rod Turner, Ted Wise, Chuck Girard, and Gene Cotton, but the real musical soul of the movement lies in the countless lesser-known groups, like the Salt Company, connected with coffeehouses, churches, and communes, which create new songs and new gospel sounds.

The new kind of gospel music ranges from hard rock, with its battering atonal rhythms, to tunes suggesting folk hymns of virtually nineteenth century sweetness. The music evokes both the contemporaneity and nostalgia aspects of the movement. The alienation of the movement as pop culture from the "great tradition" of church music is clear: there are no overtones of Palestrina, Handel, or even Arthur Sullivan. The lyrics show the same pop transformation. Commonly based on biblical phrases or stories, they contemporize the Scripture by putting it, and the singer's amazed response, in the "hip" idiom of pop music.

There is much repetition of phrases and a covert anti-intellectualism. ("Jesus is good enough for a simple singer like me.") But as in all lyrics since the advent of the Beatles, the poetry is fresh and on occasion surprisingly effective.

EXPERIENCES IN THE MOVEMENT

I attended a typical Bible class, or "Jesus rap," on a weekday night in 1971 at a "Jesus house" in a large city. It was sponsored not by a church, but by an independent group which also puts out one of the better-known throwaway papers. The leader of the session was a clean-cut intense evangelical Christian, suggesting a younger Billy Graham. Another worker in the house, of the same stamp but with longer hair, was playing a guitar. An elderly lady was fervent about saying "Praise the Lord" and handing everyone who came in a Bible. A black lady of many years had six grandchildren in tow. And there was a scattering of young people.

As the people in the group introduced themselves, the diversity of backgrounds became evident. A young black lady asked for prayers for her husband in the Air Force in a distant state and for government transportation to join him. A young man with a Prince Valiant haircut had just been converted in Sweden (of all places) where he had gotten into a pentecostal group.

The meeting opened with hymns accompanied by the guitar. This was followed with prayer, led by the leader in a warm, soft, intense, slightly stumbling manner. We prayed for the government transportation, we thanked God for the conversion in Sweden. The younger black lady said something like "Alleluia, Blood of Jesus" over and over, slowly and firmly, like a mantic formula. She said "I rebuke you in the name of Jesus" to any evil spirits present, including spirits of depression and heaviness. Someone else added spirits of sickness to the exorcism, saying that a Christian doesn't have to be sick to have any of that "trash of Satan."

The elderly white lady named a young man who was a "worshipper of Satan" for prayer, but the guitar player said that he had been with him for about three hours that afternoon, and that he had accepted Jesus. He'd met him on the street, they had walked to the Jesus center together, the Satanist had said "I'm going to fight you," but finally had given in, saying "I can't fight any longer." Everyone greatly rejoiced in these tidings, but the convert was prayed for anyway, since he would need much sustaining in his new faith. Apparently he had also been attracted to Buddhism, for they asked also that he might worship through Jesus rather than Buddha, "For Buddha said, 'I know the way,' but Jesus said, 'I am the Way,' " which got much favorable response in Alleluias and "Praise Jesus."

The meeting then moved to praising, clapping, and speaking in tongues, all starting and stopping together rather abruptly. The elderly black woman gave a message of God speaking directly through her, a message of reassurance and love—the immediate words of God! The group then sang "Gimme that Old Time Religion."

A Bible class on the topic of forgiveness, led by the young man with knitted brows with a sincerity that reminded me of Billy Graham, was next. He seemed to like to use illustrations from his childhood—fights, a brother borrowing another's clothes, and so forth. He said that he now lived in a place with two other fellows and questions arose about who would wash the dishes. He became very animated. He told of a man who came into the Jesus center with his arm broken out in terrible sores because he had been unable to forgive ... he might be dead now. In all the talk of this group, the physical expression of spiritual reality was very concrete in miracle, sickness, health. A powerful love of evangelical conversion accounts was evident. *The Cross and the Switchblade* of Dave Wilkerson was cited as a great classic of conversion stories.

An observer sensed a deep intensity, a tumultous spiritual struggle wrought out of guilt, loneliness, and yearning behind the flashed smiles, the happy greeting of everyone with "Praise the Lord," the half-ritualized emotions, the "highs" of praise and glossalalia.

The kind of background which can lie behind this coiled feeling is clear from the personal narratives of some members of the movement. Here is the story of a young man who is now a member of the commune connected with Tony and Sue Alamo's Christian Foundation. He is a husky, affable man and often drives the bus which takes street people from Hollywood Boulevard out to the services at the Foundation.

He was born in New York of an upper-middle-class Jewish family. He says that as a boy he "had everything"—high I.Q., good schools, a scholarship to New York University. But he had rebelled against authority in an almost pathological way. He got in trouble in school, joined street gangs, was a "punk." He had his first arrest in high school, and also started taking drugs at that time. First it was cough medicine with codeine, then marijuana. He stole LSD and took it and tried heroin once or twice.

By now he had gotten into the psychedelic movement. He says, however, that at first he didn't even realize the spiritual aspects of LSD; it was "just like getting drunk." However, he did participate in some fringe cultural aspects of psychedelica; he wrote poetry and went to underground movies. But generally he saw the psychedelic people as "phonies" in their professing of peace and love. He thought that "reality" was just this life and then you were six feet deep. You might as well "groove" through it, making the body feel good. So he went more and more to heroin, which doesn't promise mysticism, just a good feeling. Nonetheless he also tried the I Ching, Kabbala, Tarot cards, and Zen. His parents sent him to psychologists, then when that failed threw him out of the house. He became an out and out heroin addict. He says the psychiatrists just gave him an excuse for his behavior—he was a "sick kid." He had bitter hatred for his parents. He said also that he believed in some spiritual reality, but that he couldn't reach it, and that there was no afterlife.

He began dealing and stealing to support his drug habit. He became violent and carried a pistol in his pocket. He would have been capable, he says, of killing. He went to Europe by robbing to get the money. He married an English girl just so he could become a registered addict. Heroin was his god, his money, his girlfriend, his car. Forgetting his wife, he wandered about, still addicted to heroin.

He finally returned to America and decided to come to California. He thought he could break the habit if he got into a different environment, but it didn't work. In Los Angeles he got together with addict friends. He says that he didn't care about anything, didn't fear the police, and was full of hatred.

One day as he was walking down Sunset Boulevard on his way to the Playboy Club he ran into some gospellers from the Christian Foundation. He listened to them and got a tract, but said he had something else to do. They offered him a free meal, though, and he decided to go with them.

The first thing that struck him was that these people were *alive* and *smiling.* In the drug scene, he hadn't had feelings. When he tried to cry, or tried to laugh, he couldn't do it. He put his "tough guy" attitude ahead of feelings. But these people had emotions; somehow he liked that.

Then they said that Jesus Christ would be back and would destroy the earth. They said that God wasn't like what you thought, all forgiving like a good Grandpa. There was judgment and a burning pit of hell, and if you were ashamed of Jesus, he would be ashamed of you. He was struck by this. He had thought that Christians were "square, the most wishy-washy people on earth." But these people were *bold.*

At the center and during the service, he was told that if you say the prayer, you will *feel* the power of God. He wanted to feel it physically. He said to himself that that would be reality. If he felt something, he'd know there was a God. In drugs sensations had been a mere euphoria, floating feelings, with no gutty laughter, crying, or love. Then he said the prayer, and he felt what he had hoped to feel. It was the power of God, unspeakable and full of glory.

He left everything to join the Foundation. He forgot about drugs. He knew he was saved. His heart softened. He cried again—it was so good to have emotions. He had never before really been happy, but now he was *so happy* and *saved.* He says he has been at the Foundation two years, and he witnesses twenty-four hours a day. He called his mother to wish her a happy Mother's Day. His family was so impressed that they came out to visit him in his new life. His parents and sister became saved too, and his sister is now a member of the Foundation also.

Another young man, now also a member of the Christian Foundation, was born in Maryland of a Roman Catholic family. He says that he was not much impressed with his father's religiosity; he would often curse with the Lord's name while fighting traffic on the way home from mass.

His father was a Pentagon employee, and, like many of his generation, this young man grew up around the world, attending American schools in Okinawa and elsewhere overseas. He got good grades in school, but in high school, back in Maryland, he rebelled. He began drinking a lot with friends, stayed away from home for days at a time, and quarrelled with his father. By the age of fifteen he had spent a whole summer, independently, at the beach. At sixteen he was introduced to marijuana, and then to LSD. His psychedelic experience led him in the direction of nature mysticism; he would walk in the woods "talking to trees." In this period, he dropped out of high school a month before graduation. That summer he took LSD every day. He appreciated the "spiritual" aspect of the drug experience, but he found that *people* began to "freak him out." He couldn't stand closed places, and when he was on drugs he would go outdoors in the middle of the night. He thought going back to nature was the "right thing"—he was revolted by how man has polluted the world.

Even though he says that while on acid he "laughed at everything all the time," he was depressed within. He lived only to take acid. He couldn't communicate with anyone. When he went to church he got only cold stares.

So he decided to leave. On a plane trip to Texas, he took LSD. On this trip, he says, he "about died." He saw horrible faces and heard dreadful voices. Once in Texas, he determined to get away from people and "go back to the earth." He went to Big Sur in California. In his chronic instability, however, that didn't last either, and he moved on to Los Angeles. He couldn't work and quit every job he had. Once he went to a "love-in" that turned into a riot, and he was arrested. After this he was "really down."

Then one afternoon he was walking down the street. He met a "nice guy" and a girl who called him "wicked." He couldn't see why. But they talked about a God of wrath and a Jesus Christ who hated drugs. Almost in spite of himself, he went to their service. He noted that people had smiles and enthusiasm and that they seemed happy. They said "Praise the Lord." He had never seen anything like that in a church before. His previous impression was that unless you were a church member or had money, the church wasn't interested in you, and that if you had long hair, you couldn't be a Christian. Here he heard testimonies which gave him a different point of view. He heard Tony Alamo, who had been a Jew and an atheist, tell how Jesus had talked to him "in a supernatural way." He heard that God hated sin, but would forgive the sinner, which was why Jesus had died on the cross.

"A brother" asked him if he wanted to be saved, and he "went up to see what it felt like." He said the sinner's prayer. The effect was so fast he hardly remembers just how it happened, he says, but it was like the windows being opened suddenly in a dark smokey room. He knows it was God because it took away from him not only the need for LSD but also the desire for it. He was and is very impressed with Tony and Sue Alamo because they have actually given their lives to getting people like himself off the streets. He was taught to pray, to sing gospel songs, and so forth, and he has since seen miracles and prophecies fulfilled.

These two cases represent conversions from lives severely damaged by drug abuse. One frequently hears of cases like these, and, however they be interpreted, they certainly represent the most impressive and dramatic fruits of the Jesus movement. Groups such as the Christian Foundation, working chiefly with street people, specialize in drug conversions. The key to the conversion is characteristically the same as in these examples: an intense feeling, equal in intensity to the drug experience but different in quality, facilitates the radical transference. The continuing participation in the Jesus activity must be as all-consuming, as full-time, as drugs are for the person with an extreme dependency on them.

However, there are other kinds of Jesus people too. Here is the case of another young man with a background in the same general "youth culture," but without the same total attachment to drug experiences. He was converted at Calvary Chapel, the large youth and movement-oriented church in Orange County. He was a college student at the time of my interview with him, and he said that he is liberal from the standpoint of much of the movement. He admitted there is a lot of the Bible he cannot understand. Others always talk about the rapture, the Second Coming, and so forth, but he thinks this looking forward is not good; it's more important to live life now. But he holds that Jesus *is* the Son of God, a belief he received from Calvary Chapel, and it is central to him.

Asked just what Jesus is to him, he said that he is an image in his mind, more an understanding. "He is not all power but just everything."

Like the others, he had used marijuana and other hallucinogens, and had had some spiritual experiences from them. But he ended up with only confused feelings and so quit drugs. He picked up a copy of the *Hollywood Free Paper,* thought about it, and put his mind on Jesus. After first trying a meditation organization, he quit when he found that all he realized in meditation was that he wasn't happy.

Then he went to Calvary Chapel with some friends. The services, with their lively music and orthodox atmosphere, were not what he had expected. He had thought that at a youth-oriented church there would be a lot of people smoking pot. But there the Bible was taken as literal truth. At the altar call he felt moved to accept Christ, and he started reading the Bible and finding it filled a lot of empty spots in his life. Since then he's been the happiest he's ever been.

He has kept his own ideas on Christianity's meaning, though. He says that many in the movement feel there's much difference between Christians and non-Christians and want to think they've got something nobody else has. He's not sure there's that much difference, and after college religion classes he's not sure everything in the Bible is true. But Jesus is strong; kids on drugs sacrifice much of their lives to get "high"; Jesus gets you to the same place. It proves itself; Jesus people seem more real, always happy, not phony.

He now goes to the Christian Life Church in Long Beach, another movement church. Here the baptism of the Holy Spirit, which gives the gift of tongues, is taught, although participation in "tongues" activity is voluntary. He says he had convinced himself that speaking in tongues was impossible. But at a certain Bible class he was attending everyone else was receiving the baptism of the Holy Spirit. He was "going nuts about this"—and then received it himself.

After going to this church he has really felt the presence of God. In a church where everyone speaks in tongues, praises, and the like, it all seems so real he says he nearly faints, feels weak and drained, but happy and at peace. In that Bible class these emotions were so strong he collapsed and other people did too.

THE MOVEMENT AND THE EVANGELICAL ALTERNATIVE WORLD

The Jesus movement is the sum of a great number of intense, diverse, deeply personal experiences such as these. In all of them there has been a strong reaching, as out of deep waters, for the Jesus of the evangelical tradition. There is a fascination with the powers claimed for this Jesus, for his absolutism, for the terminology and music and customs of this tradition, for the mystique of its "holy fool," the streetcorner evangelist. Out of all this comes participation in the evangelical alternative world.

The relation of the movement to the drug culture is clear. Many of its strong adherents have passed through that initiation into transcendent experience. However disruptive of an ordered kind of life drugs may be, and however confusing spiritually, they do at least convince young people who take them that spiritual issues are real. There really are euphoric states of consciousness that compare to ordinary living as sun to shadow, and there are fierce demonic terrors which crouch in its depths. Evangelical Christianity dwells in this same terrain, but its transcedent sun is Jesus, and he has the power to cast out the demons. To evangelical Christianity belongs the same intense feeling and the same defiance of those who do not share the world of spiritual realities. Both, centering on feelings and visions beyond the prosaic, may be called romantic. But it is a pop romanticism. The two sides, the drug and Jesus cultures, are bound together not only by feeling-oriented assumptions, but also by the personal narratives of persons who have moved from one to the other. Like Alcoholics Anonymous, the Jesus movement is tied to the psychology of its greatest enemy. It thrives by bringing others out of the same hell of chemical dependence. Just as A. A. favors the coffee-klatsch, business-suit world of the middle-class alcoholic to whom it caters, so the havens of the Jesus movement carry over the dress and aura of posters and popular music of the obverse culture. Like A. A. it makes much of personal accounts of the transitional conversion event. And as A. A. does, it generates a genuine feeling of great spiritual power sufficient to meet a very real spiritual-chemical foe.

It may be unlikely that the Jesus movement will survive the drug culture as an independent cultural form. Already, as the popularity of hard drugs and the runaway psychedelic culture of the 1960s fades, the 1970 style of the Jesus movement is passing. It is being more and more taken over by churches like Calvary Chapel, or becoming sectarian. Movement churches and countless young people's groups across the land are using its symbols and speaking in tongues. But these are people like our last example, who, though they may have smoked pot once or twice, were never runaways or "heads."

4

The Transcendence of Time

TIME AND RELIGION

A TOUCHSTONE OF MEANING IN ANY RELIGION is its handling of man's experience of living in time. In the series of endless moments of which time is composed, things happen one after the other and few of them seem really fulfilling. We are frustrated because the present is always vanishing, good things remembered from the past seem locked in that past, and the future promises hopes that seem always still around the corner. We seek in religion ultimate transformation of self and world to a state where all that is good in all these moments comes together.

Different religions deal with the frustrations of time in different ways and hold out different models for transcendence of its limitations. As we have seen, evangelicalism in general endeavors to collapse the historical (and personal) stream into the immediacy of its alternative world, the world of the New Testament. We have seen that this is almost a mystical experience, but one not attained, like classical mysticism, by techniques of meditation.

Within evangelicalism several models or archetypes for evangelical transcendence of time through assimilation of the alternative world occur: movement in the miraculous New Testament world as contemporary, ecstatic loss of those rational "thinking" aspects of the mind which hold us in the time stream, vision of the present world as permeated with purposes continuous with those of the New Testament, and stress on the imminent end of the present age. In this chapter we shall look at some Jesus movement services with a view to seeing what archetypal model they hold up against the problem of time. In each case, an image of an archetypal *person* which, it is implied, the believer wants to be like, emerges. It may be the childlike believer to whom marvellous things happen and who is greater even than parents, or the woman beloved of the Lord, or the responsible patriarchal father, or the penitent at the end of his rope who accepts all accusations against him.

CALVARY CHAPEL

Probably the best known of all the Jesus people churches is Calvary Chapel in Orange County, California. For some reason it is usually said to be in Costa Mesa, but it is actually on the Santa Ana side of the street which separates the two suburban cities. Calvary Chapel was founded as an independent church by the Reverend Charles Smith in the midsixties. In 1969, at the time the present sanctuary was built, a group of a dozen young people met in it for Bible study. By 1971 hundreds if not thousands were attending meetings every night of the week. Most meetings have to be held in a large circus tent on a vacant lot a block from the church.

I attended a service on a Wednesday night, an evening devoted to the instruction of "new Christians." The fleets of folding chairs covering the asphalt floor of the tent were perhaps half filled, indicating an attendance, according to my estimate, of just under a thousand. While this is impressive, it must be remembered that Calvary Chapel draws attendance from an area with a total population of several million. On Saturday nights a "Jesus rock" concert with the evening service fills the tent.

Most of those in attendance were young people of high school and college age, dressed in the diverse costumes of their kind: patched levis, print maxis, and ample hair. Underneath, all looked like well-fed, well-scrubbed suburban youth. Nearly all had a Bible of some sort. I did not see a single non-Caucasian. Here and there was a suited, clean-shaven middle-aged man, or a bewigged and benignly smiling matron—probably curious and approving parents, or church folk supporting this good work by their presence, or visiting ministers seeking to learn the secret of Calvary Chapel's success.

The tent, lighted by an overhead rigging of electric lights and cords, was heated by great oil drums red hot from noisy compressed gas fires.

While not exactly nineteenth century, this rather delightful air of improvisation about the tent gave it all the camp meeting's spirit of breaking with the institutionalism of the parish church. When the long-discussed plans to replace the tent with a new and larger sanctuary materialize, Calvary may well find the change counterproductive for evangelism.

The service started a few minutes before the set time of 7:30. A bearded young man in white jeans and a striped sweater like a French sailor's entered to sit on a high stool on the stage. That platform held a wealth of sound equipment and musical instruments, but no religious symbols, not even a cross or open Bible. The young man began strumming a guitar and singing a song about Jesus. The crowd clapped enthusiastically along with him. Between songs he let fall a scattering of comments and messages. He sang a song about the King's Highway and said that a "highway thing" was on his mind.

He reported that recently when he was driving on the freeway, he had started speeding and had prayed to the Lord there would be no patrolman around. Then the Lord told him that this was wrong; he should "obey every ordinance of man" whether or not an officer was in sight. Then he made a wrong turn and lost twenty minutes, just the amount of time he had gained by speeding, indicating that "what a man sows that shall he reap."

This virtually karma-like experience of the immediacy of Scripture truth and God's retributive action was augmented by a story illustrating the immediacy of miracle, for Jesus people, even in the midst of this modern world. The story was second-hand, but impressive nonetheless. Two "brothers" were hitchhiking on the highway. Although they had stood by the road for several hours, "just praising the Lord," they had not gotten a ride. Recalling a Christian who had told them about a vision she had had of an angel, they decided to pray. Kneeling beside the road and placing their hands on the pavement, they prayed for an angel. They sensed the prayer was heard and that an angel stood on the highway just where they had placed their hands. A big truck then came barrelling down the highway. It roared through where the angel was standing; the Christians winced at the thought of it being crushed. But suddenly the driver put on the brakes, backed up, and gave the pair a lift. As they got into the cab he was scratching his head in bewilderment; he said he never stopped to pick up hitchhikers and had no idea why he did this time. The two said that the same technique worked to get them an early ride the next time they hit the road.

So the service opened with songs and discourses of this type as the oildrums flared and glowed. The atmosphere was casual; while most of the audience was quite attentive, people were always coming and going. A girl in a long red dress like that of a pioneer belle came out with a guitar. She sang several lovely songs of her own composition, mostly in the words of Scripture with haunting folksy melodies in the Joan Baez manner. She said that none of the songs were easy to write, for each came out of a tribulation she had been through. In the end, though, the Scripture had provided an answer; what is given in adversity like this really goes deep in the heart. She also told the story of seeing a blind girl on her college campus with a companion feeling flowers. The sightless one said she wanted to touch the "dull" flowers, those blooms which were soft and appealing to the fingers. Somehow this reminded our speaker of the Scriptural verse, "Now we see through a glass, darkly; but then face to face."

The next singer-speaker was a smiling young blond fellow with the look of a beach boy. He told us his own version of the story of the three pigs, which the Lord wanted him to relate that evening, even though he had prepared something else. Each of the three pigs told the mother pig what he planned to do in life. The first wanted to go to a mountain shack with his girl friend and a store of food and drink. The second planned to go to the city and "make a killing." The third had just "taken Jesus into his heart" and had not presumed to make any plans, saying he would pray and wait upon the Lord's guidance, intending in the meantime to stay around home. This greatly disconcerted the mother pig, for she confided that she and the father pig had only been staying together for the sake of the children, and it was not really considerate of the youngest son not to "give her her freedom" by conveniently leaving home like the others. But the youngest pig told his mother sternly that her divorce intentions were wrong, and that he would stay to pray that she and his father might also soon find the Lord Jesus. At this point the narrator stopped to confess that the story "had no ending." There was gentle laughter, but I had a feeling something about the story was probably uncomfortably familiar to many of the listeners.

The same speaker also mentioned a current tragedy. In another California town, a psychologist had shot his wife, children, cats, and himself. He reminded the audience that the night before, on TV, the room of the murdered fourteen-year-old daughter had been shown. She was a Christian; in the room the cameras picked up a cross and a poster saying "Jesus has a lot to give." We offered deep prayers for all involved in this matter.

The transition to the sermon was made by singing a series of low, soft chant-like hymn verses. There were no formal announcements, and no collection was taken. But the young assistant minister in white jeans who gave the main message started with a plug for Chuck Smith's prophecy class on Thursday night. He then went into a rather unexpected talk about his dealings in Hollywood on behalf of a record called "Love Song" being put out by the church. He indicated that, even though he knew nothing of that crass and cynical world, his trust in God gave him freedom and confidence there, opening doors both for the record and for witnessing. "Where the Spirit of God is, there is perfect liberty." God is your Father, your Dad, he said; if you goof, he'll forgive you, and you're not responsible to anyone else, not to your parents, to the government, to business, or to Satan. The Christian is free of debilitating entanglements and so has the joy of true liberty. As an example of God's influence in Hollywood, he told of a record promoter who wanted to distribute several thousand copies of the record to disc jockeys together with a copy for each of a recently issued edition of the Bible with pictures of the Christian life at Calvary Chapel interspersed throughout the text. The assistant minister leapt at this opportunity to sow the seed of the Word as well as promote the record—also of course an evangelistic vessel. Needless to say, there were numerous expressions of wonder and interjections of "Praise the Lord" amid the narration of these movements of grace.

He then started the sermon proper, which was about the Transfiguration and revealed something of the deeper things of Christian spirituality. The listeners were soon caught up in the glory of the Christian's closeness to Christ, who is in turn close to God. Alluding to 1 Corinthians 2:16, "We have the mind of Christ," the preacher repeated several times, "You can have the mind of the Son of God." He spoke of God's wisdom, given liberally to all who ask. He told us that as Christians we go boldly near the throne of God; we are with God forever. "The Christian's lows are still higher than anyone else's highs."

Afterwards, the service ended fairly swiftly. The Lord's Prayer was sung in unison. Then, after prayer, everyone was asked to bow his head and those who now made a decision for Christ were asked to raise their hands. Fifteen did so. They were asked to meet with the assistant pastor for just four or five minutes for instruction and to receive a free Bible. Anyone else who wanted a free Bible was requested to go to a different part of the room. An "Afterglow Service" was announced for those who wished to stay. It included quiet praise and speaking in tongues.

Several little clues helped establish the tone of the service. Leaders and congregants alike made such frequent use of expressions like "Praise the Lord" and "God bless you" that it seemed almost ritual. In prayer many would point one finger upward, or raise both hands.

MANSION MESSIAH

The atmosphere of the meeting continued and intensified at a commune affiliated with Calvary Chapel called Mansion Messiah. It is located in a big old house on a mostly commercial street in Costa Mesa, between a gas station and a firewood lot. Calvary Chapel has three other communes, including Philadelphia House on the beach.

Mansion Messiah has had as many as 40 members, and will house 30 comfortably. At the time I visited it in early 1972, however, only twelve people were living there. I was told that the reason for the decline was that most stay there for only six months or so after conversion, and that many had grown strong enough in the Word to leave on their own to do the Lord's work elsewhere. Some in the commune are new Christians who had been through drugs and the counter culture, though the "deacon" and a friend who showed me around had been previously in an Assemblies of God Bible college in Texas. They had felt they were just receiving and not giving in that situation. Hearing about the Jesus movement on the Coast, they had ventured west and had been in Mansion Messiah for about a month.

Men live on the first floor and women on the second, except for the "elder," who is married and lives on the second with his wife and three children. The furniture was old but comfortable, and there was little of the grubby atmosphere often present in some youth communes. The beds were made and the floors were spotless; everything was shipshape. Few books were in evidence except Bibles, but they were scattered everywhere, along with volumes on prophecy. I was presented with an autobiographical book by a Dutchman who smuggled Bibles behind the Iron Curtain. All except two or three of the members of Mansion Messiah have outside work, generally at such jobs as driving cars for used car lots. All income is pooled, and much of the food and equipment is donated by church friends.

The backyard of the house was taken up largely by a volleyball court. The garage held a fine assortment of gardening and carpentry tools, most of them gifts. In back of the garage, facing the alley and the gas station, was a curious row of compartments. Like six or eight doghouses set side by side, each compartment was a cell about four feet high and three feet wide. Each was just large enough for a kneeling person, and had a door which locked from the inside. Each was completely bare except for carpeting on the floor. Light and air were admitted only by a few very narrow slits in the door. These are prayer rooms, where members of the commune can retire for devotions. It is a practical idea for a religious community whose members have no privacy since several of them share each bedroom. Yet I was reminded of the tiny cave-cells of ancient Buddhist monks I have seen in Japan and central Asia.

The group kindly asked me to take supper with them. Two things impressed me as I talked with them: the unceasing smiles and the unceasing talk of prophecy. This group shared a strong expectation that these are the last days. The mood was reinforced by the few books around, which seemed to run to commentaries on the Book of Revelation and applications of Bible prophecies to the present day. They generally assumed that virtually all prophecy of what would occur before the Day of the Lord had been fulfilled, and that every curse of the present day, from the atomic bomb to the walking catfish plague in Florida, was connected with the impending "tribulations." Some of the smiling dinner table group said, "I'll give the world five years." Others said, "I don't think we'll see 1975." Like all Jesus people, they were always smiling, yet oddly reticent folk. They failed to reveal much about themselves except what can be put in standardized evangelical language: sin, conversion, assurance, challenge. The rough edges of personality and individuality had been cut and trimmed to the mold for the sake of the greater bounty which oneness with a common archetype yields. We talked about the value of the study of prophecy. Even though some things in religion might be even more important, we concluded, mulling over prophecy can keep the reader watchful, not mentally conformed to this passing world, but close to the Word.

The baptisms in the ocean held by Calvary Chapel have become virtually a symbol of the Jesus movement in the national press. Pictures of attractive girls in bikinis arising out of the baptismal waters radiant with joy make splendid magazine photographs. As many as a thousand have been baptized at one of these events, held every month or two. However there is no systematic preparation or follow-up for candidates who experience the ocean baptism. Calvary Chapel has little use for formal requirements, lists, or certificates. Many attending the mass baptism with friends decide on the spur of the moment to enter the waters. Undoubtedly some then start attending the nightly classes in the tent, and others are never seen again. It all depends, so far as Calvary Chapel is concerned, not on the machinery of church bureaucracy, but on the fast or slow, but always humanly inexplicable, workings of grace.

THE CHURCH IN LOS ANGELES

Another unconventional church which has been gathering sizable numbers of young Christians is simply called The Church in Los Angeles. Even more than Calvary Chapel, its worship suggests both an apocalyptic separation from the world and a collapse of time into immediate ecstasy. This church draws its origins from a movement started by a Chinese ex-Methodist minister called Watchman Nee, who died in 1972 at the age of seventy-one. In the 1930s and 1940s he founded hundreds of churches in China based on what he believed was a strictly New Testament model. Disciples establishes similar congregations in other countries. Many of those started in North America later vanished, though churches still exist in San Francisco, Los Angeles, Fresno, Yerba Linda, California, and in Vancouver, B.C. The Los Angeles church was reestablished in 1962 in a new location with a remodelled polity. Originally about one-third Chinese, the congregation is now only about 5 percent oriental. This is partly because it has been growing very quickly, especially among young people. Most of the members, however, are not truly new Christians but converts from traditional Christian churches who came to feel the church of their former allegiance was misguided. Some ministers who have lost souls to the Church in Los Angeles call it parasitical.

The Church in Los Angeles has "witnessed" by means of impressive parades of more than a thousand persons, either of young people or of adults, wearing white garments and carrying big banners. On several occasions these demonstrations in Los Angeles, MacArthur Park, have attracted much attention and newspaper stories. But the church does not advertize or even have any sign or steeple on its plain attractive building.

The Church has no paid ministers, though it does have "elders." At least ostensibly, decisions are made by consensus and church work done by volunteers as they are moved by the Spirit. Anyone who wants to work in the office is welcome to do so. Anyone who wants to conduct nursery school for the children during meetings may do so. Members come to the building during the week to mow the lawn, change light bulbs, do painting, or sweep. The Church claims some 600 members, about half of whom live in an informal community around the building, and support the nightly two-or-three-hour-long Bible study and service. They form a very tight group.

Visiting a Sunday morning service, I entered a plain large room with folding chairs arranged in concentric circles. No cross or picture ornamented the austere hall. Several hundred people were there, many young, many with foreign appearance or accent. I thought of the church in the Book of Acts, with its motley collection of peoples, its meetings in homes and catacombs, its being simply known as "the Church in" this or that city.

The structure of the service was much like that of early Quakers. Anyone who felt like testifying, teaching, or starting a song did so. The meeting began on the theme of Living Waters. We sang the old hymn "Drinking at the Fountain." A man shouted, "We've got to stop thinking and start drinking." The anti-intellectual motif was picked up by others. The natural mind, we heard, is how Satan gets in. The Devil comes in through one's thoughts. Hydraulic imagery was used for one's capacity for grace; we have the pipes and taps all set up, all we need to do is turn them on. It is not by religion, or Christianity, or tradition, as received in the churches, that this is done, however. Throughout the exchange people gave "testimonials," which were often just "Alleluia," "Praise the Lord," "Jesus," or "Amen." Frequently the word would be picked up by the others and would be chanted over and over in unison, until every drop of feeling had been drained from it.

The congregation turned to the story in the Gospel of John of the Samaritan woman at the well whom Jesus met and asked for a drink, offering her in exchange "a spring of water welling up to eternal life." Jesus then told her correctly that she had had five husbands, and that "the hour is coming, and now is, when the true worshiper will worship the Father in spirit and in truth," for "God is spirit." Under the guidance of an ad hoc leader, they read the passage through verse by verse, in unison, saying "Amen, Praise Lord Jesus" after each verse. "Discussion" consisted of simply throwing out a verse, and then from around the room came "free association" replies. For example, the leader said, in a loud voice, "He must needs go through Samaria!" and a response came, "There is a Samaria in ourselves . . ." The word was, "The well was deep." The answer was that "Christianity" says you need cranking and a rope—study, effort, application—to get the water, but the true Christ is a living fountain springing up. (The man who answered in this way said he had formerly been a Seventh-Day Adventist.) The words "springing up" were mouthed in an emotional, mantic way. They were picked up by the group and repeated over and over rhythmically.

The feeling of the superiority of anti-rational simplicity was reinforced by these chants, and by the simple, tinsely hymns. One was sung to the tune of "Jingle Bells." As we continued through the passage to the words of the woman at the well whom Jesus perceived to be an adultress, one man, to some friendly laughter, said over and over her words, "I have a husband, I have a husband . . ."

An elder arose to speak at length. He said we are all women, Christ is the bridegroom, the true husband, who wants to drink with us and make love with us. Other things—wife, children, jobs, possessions—are false husbands. They chanted, "Get rid of the husbands, get rid of the husbands . . ."

Before God, the elder said, we are women. Women are "dependent," the "weaker vessel" ("There is no women's lib in the Church"), and "crave satisfaction." We should all be like this toward Christ. He radically contemporanized the New Testament: the "inward" meaning is that all those who met Christ in John's Gospel—Nicodemus, the blind man, the Samaritan woman, Lazarus—are *"you and me."*

Christ then wants to drink from us. What he asked of the woman, water, he asks from us. As we drink deep, deep from Christ, he drinks of us and the fountain of living water gushes up within us. It is an exchange: he gets in us and needs us as we need him.

Christ is the *life*. To the Church in Los Angeles, Christ would seem to be a name for the peak experience, for intensity of feeling. One man said, "If we're honest, we are not feeling anything most of the time. But we can be—it is trying to spring up within us."

This service clearly released feelings which allowed archetypal images, male-female antagonisms, childhood delights, and deeply repressed sexual and anticomplexity drives to rise to the surface of the mind. Thus Jesus is the true husband and the gushing fountain. He is the husband who won't disappoint but will really give ecstatic experience. Toward him we must all be weak, dependent, craving satisfaction. The fountain no doubt also represents the waters of rebirth, but rebirth too is an experience closely related to the psychology of the feminine. The double meaning of the repetition of the "drinking" motif—intoxication and spiritual rapture—is also evident. The Bible words are always interior, with no historical or intellectual perspective. (Samaria is within. "It doesn't matter," someone said, "whether or not you know where Sychar is.")

Another leader, a mathematics teacher by profession, told us that contrary to the teachings of "Christianity," God the Father, Jesus, and the "Life" are not separate but one. "Christianity" makes it teaching and act, but instead it is "New Life." Jesus doesn't "give" the "Life" as a gift, but comes himself. To get one of these three, you must get all three.

In this service the experience of Jesus as ecstatic rejection of all conditioning by time, both historical and psychological, was supremely clear. Unlike the conversation at Mansion Messiah, here was not even any excited talk about the imminent coming of Jesus. It was simply *now,* whenever you turn on the tap of your spiritual plumbing to allow Jesus, as true water and true husband, to give himself to you in a virtual spiritual orgasm. This mood is not wholly typical of the Jesus movement, nor is The Church in Los Angeles really a movement church, though it draws many young people. But it is worth consideration because it illustrates vividly the ecstatic *Jesucentric* rapture which is one important side of its experience.

SHARING THE SUFFERINGS OF GOD'S PEOPLE

I could not help comparing that experience to the sermon at the evening service at an evangelically oriented church of a mainline denomination which I attended the same day. Although this church has played a very constructive role in the Jesus movement, this service was not primarily oriented toward young people.

The service began as people were asked to turn to their neighbors and say something, to open themselves up for a minute without giving name or job. An elderly lady told me how many people she had gotten to her church class. Then those who wished were asked to give testimonies about what Jesus had done for them. A secretary had gotten a better job at $750 a month, a teacher had been led to attend an evangelistic meeting. We were asked to pray for those who needed help, including a college boy who divided his time between a Jesus movement communal house and a fraternity, and who was sometimes deeply interested in God's love, but sometimes was so far from grace as to get drunk with his fraternity brothers.

After this the sermon was on Hebrews 11: 23–29. This passage summarizes how Moses sacrificed his life in Egypt to do the hard but necessary task of leading God's people, which had been laid upon him. These verses encapsulate admirably the concept of deferred reward. Moses gave up pleasure and mystical ecstasy alike in the present in order to live in historical time and obey God's word. It is such long-range planning and task orientation which The Church in Los Angeles obviously negates in favor of ecstatic immediacy.

The preacher began the sermon on a sensuous note—he told of Pharaoh's young daughter swimming in the Nile and seeing the "pretty naked baby" floating in the basket. But the message was that one cannot return to that. He laid great stress on Moses' "refusing the pleasures of sin for a season in order to share the sufferings of God's people." He talked of the splendor of Moses' decision and the fact that, dying before he could cross over into the Promised Land, he never got much of an earthly reward. It appeared the deferred reward sacrifice is a reward in itself.

This minister was clean-shaven, wore a dark suit and tie, and mentioned in passing watching TV with his children. A seminarian who led a prayer in the service, and who clearly was trying to identify with the Jesus movement generation, was casually dressed and couched his petitions in childish slang like "sharing is neat." I was struck with the generational change in Christian rhetoric: in the course of the evening the Christian moved from identification with the patriarch to identification with the child, even as that morning we had identified with the feminine in our psyches. In any case, it appeared that the sense of time and historical movement enjoyed by Moses and the Calvinist of old, careful of his morals and his purse, is passing. For the movement, it is ecstasy now, and Jesus coming back very soon to shake this world.

THE CHRISTIAN FOUNDATION

That attitude is certainly the outlook of Tony and Susan Alamo's Christian Foundation, two members of which have already told their stories. Tony and Sue are both of Jewish background. Tony Alamo was born Bernie Lazar Hoffman; he took his present name when he became a professional singer. He now says, though, that in those days, and also as he later moved into successful ventures in record production and promotion and in health studios, he found no peace in his life. He says that once when he was in an attorney's office to discuss a business matter, "God came down upon me in a very supernatural way and made me know beyond any shadow of doubt the reality of his son Christ Jesus." Soon after, he was constrained to go into evangelism and the Christian Foundation work. Nonetheless, there is a distinct impression that his wife is the partner who exercises most of the leadership, just as she does most of the speaking. They do not live at the Christian Foundation, but drive in and out from an attractive home in Studio City.[16]

When I visited the Foundation in November of 1971, it happened to be the day the Foundation was 1,000 days old. A birthday cake sat in the church hall. The main building of the Foundation is a former restaurant, rustic but comfortable. A church hall and a dining room are the center to which the buses bring those attracted by the street evangelicalism in Hollywood. Visitors also receive the free meal there. Outsiders are not allowed to visit the five or six communal houses where the permanent residents live. Those who decide to stay with the Foundation spend their first week or so just reading the Bible, getting "grounded." Then they start helping with the work: gardening, witnessing on the street, driving the vehicles. The finances are handled entirely by the Alamos.

The Foundation was started with the help of the nondenominational pentecostal Full Gospel Businessmen's Association. Now the Foundation receives some $15,000 a month in donations; finances are said to be shaky, but there is always enough. In the commune, men and women live far apart. Drugs, drinking, social dancing, physical contact between the sexes, and even conversation between the sexes except in groups is forbidden, though smoking is not. Members may marry, but only after a ninety-day period of total separation for prayer and fasting for the couple. Like early Christian monasticism in its reaction against the chaotic self-indulgence of the late Roman world, it appears that this rigor and discipline appeals to some surfeited with drugs and hedonism; few people have left the apocalpytic commune.

The meeting began when Tony and Sue came to the front of the hall to open the service. Tony reminded me, in his dapper white suit with striped tie and his short-hair, clean-shaven good looks, of pictures of Rudolf Valentino. His wife, a dimpled, middle-aged blonde, was attractive with a strong-minded quality about her.

Like Calvary Chapel, this chapel was well-equipped with the electronic accoutrements of modern rock music. Several hundred people, most though not all young, were present and responded enthusiastically to the ear-splitting rock versions of gospel music. A singer sang "In the Garden" in night club style, squeezing every drop of erotic quality from it. A large choir did an ebullient rendition of the Hallelujah Chorus. After each song—and there were many—hands were raised in praise, and the clapping, dancing fervor continued into glossalalia and wordless adoration.

The ecstatic tone changed when Tony gave announcements in his flat businessman's voice. He insisted that any tracts handed out at the service had to be screened. They had to use the King James version of the Bible only and say that Jesus is coming soon. We were told that after the service baptism would be offered and that then the bus would leave for witnessing before the evening service.

Holy Communion was distributed. Sue first told of the curse which rests on those who receive Communion unworthily. There was a period of soft hymns and forgiveness before the sacrament. People moved about the room shaking hands and embracing each other, reconciling differences. In some cases it was parents and children. More than one pair of eyes were moist.

When the bread and grape juice were passed out, two girls in front would not recieve. Sue Alamo, seeing this, demanded of them the reason. They said, timorously, they were afraid they were not saved. But she loudly insisted that they kneel and confess, and then that they be served. She added, in a not unkindly voice, that the devil gets in with thoughts like those of the two girls.

The sermon was given by Sue Alamo. It was totally nonintellectual, delivered in a shrill, fiery, emotional, intensely powerful style. She said that children ask their parents and pastors, "Who is God?" They get all sorts of answers, and those who give misleading answers will hear them reverberate back at them from the Great White Throne of Judgment. The Bible says that God is not a God of permissive love, but that those who love him must love his commandments. He is not a God to reinforce what people want, but a God who is. Statements like these were greeted with applause. Sue Alamo indicated in the course of the sermon that she is praying for, and expecting soon, a "supernatural ministry," with gifts of healing and prophecy. The whole atmosphere was that of the camp meeting, with music and emotional rhetoric the main vehicles leading to confession and transformation. At the end of the sermon, several went up to be saved. One felt the confrontational tone augmented the tension-laden chaos of the lives of those at the meeting to the breaking point, and then resolved the conflict.

RESPONSES TO TIME

In this chapter we have surveyed several ways in which the language of the Jesus movement enables the believer to transcend ordinary, burdensome time. Calvary Chapel seemed to inculcate the mystical-ecstatic experience as a permanent state, by saying that you have the mind of the Son of God and that your "lows" as a Christian are still higher than anyone else's "highs," and displaying in song and story the vista of living in a marvellous Christian world of smiles, enthusiasm, rapturous praise, secrets, miracles, appearing angels, the supernatural convergence of events to make everything come out right in the end. At Mansion Messiah the stress was on time as about to end, and so unimportant, and those who are in on this secret can smile. At The Church in Los Angeles, ordinary time was swallowed up in ecstatic immediacy; the feeling intensity of each moment was supposed to be so great one simply forgot about past and future, or even analyzing why the present moment with Christ is so intensely powerful. In the sermon at the major denominational church, present time was given meaning through the possibility of its being devoted to tasks which are part of God's plan. At the Alamo's Christian Foundation, the trivial burdens of present time are blasted away by total apocalyptic confrontation with God's judgmental wrath in one's individual life and in the imminent assize from the Great White Throne. We must now look at how the responses to the individual's problem of meaninglessness in the unending series of moments, choices, experiences, and ups and downs—the burden of ordinary time—have also shaped a pattern of response to historical time.

5

Responses to History

HISTORY AND APOCALYPTIC TIME

WE HAVE REITERATED THAT A FUNDAMENTAL PROBLEM of religion is the problem of time. How is it that, on the one hand, a person experiences moments of peak experience, when time seems to fall away and only God is alive in his timeless being, and on the other hand has to return to live through time—to be born, suffer the joys and adversities of this life, grow old, and die. Moreover, with the rest of mankind, each person is under the wheel of the cruel vicissitudes of history in general, with its wars and epidemics, hopes and terrors.

Above all, life and history are just one thing after another. They cancel out virtually every mood which arises within them. Nothing conditioned by time and history is stationary. Yet if God is the Master and Maker of all things, he must be "Lord of History" too. Its pains and triumphs alike must somehow fall from his hands, as do the experiences in which the individual feels lifted out of time.

Eastern religions have responded to this conundrum by viewing temporal experience as a divine play, a round of cycles and reincarnations ultimately meaningless, save as the individual within them finds ultimate transformation into timeless consciousness outside the game. In the West the great monotheistic religions of Semitic background—

Judaism, Christianity, and Islam—have taken a different approach. With them time is linear—a straight line marked by irreversible periods and unrepeatable events starting with the creation of the world by God and ending with his final judgment. Realization of God is only partially a present possibility. Its fullness does not come until a future point, when God will judge the world and annihilate the powers of evil within it. Only then, when evil has finally been defeated, can full perfection, both of the cosmic environment and of the individual, including the capacity to know God fully, be attained. Ultimate transformation of self and world go together.

For the Western religions, then, history is not a permanent stage on which a drama without beginning or end is being played, but a temporary platform on which a short, hard-hitting play is acted beginning with the building of the stage and ending when the author walks onto it. When history is viewed in this light, it is natural that people nourished in such a tradition should from time to time wonder if the End is not near. Some like Hegel and Teilhard de Chardin have, to be sure, interpreted Judaeo-Christian eschatology (teachings about the Last Days) in an evolutionary manner. They have believed it means that the world is moving progressively toward its goal by stages through seemingly natural means, though in accordance with God's plan.

But another style of interpretation, the apocalyptic, was burning brightly at the time of the genesis of Christianity, has flared up frequently throughout its history, and is today kindled with a new vigor in the Jesus movement. It holds that times will instead get worse and worse before the End, until the years just previous to it, called the "tribulation," are of almost unendurable anguish and display the seeming victory of evil in the person of the Antichrist. Thus the days of the End are like birthpangs, most excruciating just before the new life is here.

The return of Christ at this point is a radical reversal, like his resurrection, offering joy beyond hope, joy keener than grief, just when all seems darkest. Then the powers of wickedness are dispersed like mists before the rising sun and a new heaven and earth appear, beautiful beyond the loveliest vistas of a landscape by an old Chinese master, with cities more shining than those of any futuristic fantasy.

For the apocalyptist, his scenario is the only real answer to despair and to the seeming stranglehold of evil on this world. However unlikely sounding it may be to an outsider, to him it seems better than any alternative, both on the basis of scripture and, even more profoundly though perhaps less consciously, because of the deepest anxieties and intuitions of his spiritual quest. At least for those who accept theism, the best argument for the apocalyptic world view remains that of 2 Peter

3: 5–7. If God made the world out of nothing once, there is no reason he could not make it anew. The idea of a new heaven and earth is no more unlikely than the fact that anything exists at all.

THE APOCALYPTIC VISION

Apocalyptic fervor is no new thing in the Judaeo-Christian tradition. Like a huge tide, it has risen and fallen with the centuries and millenia. As the year 1000 approached, an expectation that Christ would return in that evenly-numbered year swept Europe. Multitudes confessed tearfully and gathered in churches. In the same way, there is again great anticipation that the year 2000 will be of very special importance, for good or ill, an anticipation at least as old as the famed prophecies of Nostradamus.

It has only been in the nineteenth and twentieth centuries, however, that an apocalyptic style characteristic of the biblical period prophets and apocalypticists has been renewed. That style involves reading contemporary historical events in the light of expectations based on Scripture and vision concerning specific events believed to be indicators of the coming End. Today this pattern is certainly connected to the rise of "historicism." Ours has been an age of a radical discovery of history —the definitive discovery that events move in an irreversible sequence and can be interpreted as having a meaning which points toward the future. That is, events can be signs. The Marxist, the evolutionist, the biblical apocalypticist all have their meaning-giving pattern to lay over the puzzle of historical event.

The apocalypticist will, of course, look for events which indicate the approaching time of tribulation and the subsequent coming of Christ. He believes Scripture contains a great number of prophecies concerning what will happen in the "latter days" just before the Return, just as there were scriptural prophecies of the birth of Christ and other events. Prophecies about the End are said to be found in many places in the Bible, but especially in the books of Ezekiel, Daniel, certain chapters of the Gospels, and Revelation. Some prophetic passages predict political events, such as the ingathering of Israel and the battle of Armageddon; others allude to natural phenomena, like the darkening of the sun and moon, the falling of the stars, and the shaking of the powers of heaven.

Many social commentators have pointed out that apocalyptic thought flourishes most in times of stress and anxiety and among groups who feel themselves alienated and/or oppressed. This fits the apocalypticists' own interpretation of their situation, for certainly the time of tribulation is one of stress, and they believe the true Church is almost always oppressed. The pervasive apocalypticism of the Jesus movement, then, suits both its own nature as a social movement and also the type of person it attracts.

In regard to the definition of religion as a means of ultimate transformation of self and world, Christian apocalypticism of course offers transformation of self through evangelical conversion, but under the special stimulus of expectation of God's approaching transformation of the world. The individual, converted or not, can do little personally to affect the course of that great apocalyptic scenario, but its ongoing presence is a powerful instrument for self-transformation. One transforms himself by putting himself into the drama as an aware actor-observer. It becomes his alternative world. As he observes with passive awe the larger dimensions of the prewritten drama, he participates actively, seeking to affect the world's preparation for its end by bringing others, while there is yet time, consciously into the mighty tragicomedy as fellow actor-observers.

HAL LINDSEY AND JESUS MOVEMENT APOCALYPTIC

No apocalyptic teacher is more popular than Hal Lindsey. His book, *The Late Great Planet Earth,* is one of the few volumes besides the Bible found in virtually every movement commune, home, and church parlor.[17] Next to the Scripture, probably no other book is more read. It has shaped the pattern which the present apocalyptic expectation has taken, despite the fact that his scholarship is casual and selective by any standards—fundamentalist, traditional, or liberal—and that comparison of the passages he emphasizes with others he omits suggests that his choice of material is somewhat conditioned by his thesis. But his charming "hip" style and the obvious relevance of his vision of the future to what is happening now render his book seductively exciting.

Lindsey's method of writing is true to the almost shamanistic vocation of the prophet and apocalypticist, who has ever been another man from the pedantic textualist. Ezekiel, Daniel, and the John of the Book of Revelation were never bound to a balanced weighing out of the words of Moses in their "night visions." They made from what, to them, were older Scriptural words and images new figures, images, typologies, and predictions to express and validate what God was doing in the world. Yet the method was always a peculiarly apocalyptic style of selective literalism, far removed in mood from either a liberal metaphorical exegesis or a systematic literalistic dogmatism. Hal Lindsey, as a modern apocalyptic prophet, is one with that school when he does not hesitate to equate Meshech etymologically with Moscow, and to read atomic blasts in references to fire and brimstone. His is an apocalyptic devotion to Scripture so direct as to leave no room for distancing by time or analytic criticism, and totally involved with a passionate engagement in the anguish of the modern world. If other scholars do not derive the same message from these passages, that is because they approach them with a different purpose and different sets or presuppositions. They may be too quick to assume that the meaning of scriptural passages is exhausted by reference to their ancient contexts, and miss the possibility that they may glance off sparks in another direction when touched by the mind of a prophetic shaman.

Hal Lindsey's headquarters is a Spanish-style house a couple blocks from UCLA called the J.C. Light and Power Company. It is now a commune housing about forty-five people, around half of whom are UCLA students. The others work in the house, or have outside jobs, two or three for groups like Campus Crusade.

The house was obtained through a wealthy oil man, who also lets them use his swimming pool for baptisms. Pat Boone is also close to Hal and says he will let them use his pool for baptisms too.

Like most Christian communes, the atmosphere is one of soft smiles, clever Jesus posters, and neat rooms with conspicuous Bibles on the desks. On a visit there I talked with a converted (or, as they say, "completed") Jew who lived in the house. A bearded, older man, he said that he had been a movie stunt man and had tried all sorts of spiritual things —Eastern religions, drugs, and so forth—but didn't find peace. Then he saw Hal's book, and had to talk with him. Hal didn't give him any answers, when they conversed, but told him where he could find them in the Bible. Somehow, the prophecy approach got through to this searcher. He sold all he had and quit his career (he now has a night club job) to come and devote all his free time to studying prophecy. He is cheerful, laughs at himself, and likes to say, "I'm the craziest one here."

Two students I talked with, a tall boy who had been raised in a Covenant church but fell away, and then came back through Hal, and a girl from the South, confirmed the experience. They had all had a strong and definite experience of accepting Christ, together with a kind of follow-up illumination which made the Bible clear. But they were not necessarily charismatic or pentecostal. Rather, they were oriented to the study approach, rejecting too much emphasis on "high" experiences.

What this group seemed to have in common was a detached, prophetic, virtually contemplative concern with world events. I asked if there was any political bent to the Jesus movement. The Hal Lindsey group responded with a feeling that the whole system is corrupt. One student said he had changed from being a political science major a year ago, because he did not think it was to the point. But they rejected the notion that the movement, if only by default, strengthened the right wing. They cited Hal as saying that the right wing is just as dangerous as the left, it not more so, as a potential source of the Antichrist's demonic one-world government. I was told there were many kinds of people and lifestyles in the house, from "straight" to "hip," but that most were concerned with very detailed day-by-day analysis of world events in the light of prophecy, in an interpretive, nonactivist manner.

Hal, now about forty, did not have a strongly religious upbringing. He was raised in Texas, was in the Coast Guard, and was a Mississippi river boat pilot. He then allegedly lived a "life of sin," and his parties in New Orleans were the talk of the town. But at twenty-six he was converted and went to a fundamentalist seminary in Dallas. From then on his ministry has been increasingly oriented to prophecy.

Life in the house centers around Lindsey's famous Bible classes, particularly those on Tuesday and Wednesday nights. They are fabulously well attended and carefully taped by his avid followers—some of whom, I was told, attend no other church services. I attended one of Hal's classes in early 1972. Several hundred young people were crowded into the living room of the former fraternity house, and more overflowed into adjacent rooms, halls, and the garden. Hal stood in the center of the room holding his Bible. His round face bore the earnest, wide-eyed look of a southern country boy, and he spoke in a flat, sincere Texas drawl. The discourse was interspersed with sympathetic laughter, shouts of "Praise the Lord," and "amens" from the audience. He was talking about a recent meeting he had had with the famous psychic Jeane Dixon. While judiciously feeling that she was well meaning and that some attacks on her were unfair, he seemed to feel she was being used by unhealthy spiritual forces. The test of a real prophet, he said, is that he is 100 percent accurate, and that what he says conforms to the Word of God. These last days are times of miracles, but not all miracles are of God. We must be prepared for the wiles of Satan, who can produce good feelings too.

In his book, *The Late Great Planet Earth,* the keystone for Hal Lindsey's vision is the reestablishment of the nation of Israel in 1948. This begins the last generation, which will not taste of death before the Lord returns. (He states that a biblical generation is about forty years.) The ingathering of the Jews to the Holy Land fulfills many prophecies about the Last Days. We are now in a period of gathering storm between that inaugural event and the tribulation.

According to Lindsey, it will begin with an assault by Magog (Russia) and its Arab and African allies upon Israel. A response will be made by a ten-nation Western alliance centered in Rome and led by a dictator who is the Antichrist. During a period of authority of only three and one-half years, the Antichrist will win the worship of most people by establishing a pseudo utopia in which everyone has a number and the standard of living rises. But he will viciously persecute Christians. During his reign, 144,000 Jews will be converted to Christ and spread the gospel powerfully despite persecution from the state.

Russia and her allies (which she double-crosses) will be destroyed after a ghastly nuclear war in which most cities of the earth, and virtually the whole Russian people, are annihilated. But after only a brief pause, an army from China of 200 million will move west. It will meet the army of the Western alliance on the fateful plain of Armageddon. The frightful atomic conflict which ensues would be more than the earth could bear, were it not that it is interrupted by an even greater event: the sudden appearance of Christ. Then the Judgment will follow. Thereafter Christ will rule for a thousand years (the Millenium) over the saints on a reconstituted, paradisical earth. At the end of those ten centuries, Satan will be loosed again for a short while, and then the whole cosmos will be transfigured into the new heaven and earth, with a glory before which even the anticipatory millenium will seem pale.

It should be explained that those who were Christians before the tribulation, with all its holocausts, will not be around to suffer through it. (Those who suffer persecution under the Antichrist are the Jews, mostly converted by a direct miracle, and those missionized by them.) Those who were Christians before that will be taken up just before the tribulation, in what is called the "rapture," to return with Christ. They are envisioned by Lindsey as simply disappearing from this world. He calls the rapture "the ultimate trip."

To persons of a certain susceptibility, these thoughts provide a life of delightful anticipatory excitement. Apocalyptic happiness is a very real state, different both from the pleasures of the present life and the ecstasy of mystical experience. It is an exuberant mental picturing and fervent hoping for a new world, better than the former and more lasting than a mystical "high." It is a special spiritual state, providing a special relationship to the world. The apocalypticist accepts the fact that the world, following a sort of spiritual second law of thermodynamics, is getting worse and worse morally, in extent of suffering, and in the apparent power of evil. He knows the worst is yet to come. In fact, as though to confirm his faith, he looks for evidence of this. He is confident that the greater the sufferings, the nearer the promised reversal of all evil and breakthrough of ultimate good. While he does not exactly rejoice in the sufferings of the world, he welcomes what they signify.

(Of course, a few apocalypticists are unbalanced in the direction of a temperament which delights in alleged or real persecutions, and takes undue pleasure in the thought of the coming judgment upon the wicked.)

Apocalypticism gives interest to current events, thought it precludes any real need for commitment to political action since the destiny of the present world is already determined. The apocalypticist observes with great interest the curious pivotal place which Israel now has in world affairs. Lindsey believes that the European Common Market will be the base of the ten-nation alliance over which the Roman Antichrist will rule. The apocalyptic observer will note that, since Lindsey's book was published, the Market has grown from six to nearly ten member states. He shares in a sense of rapid-paced events moving faster and faster toward penultimate disaster—political, economic, ecological. The fact that the U.S. does not play a prominent role in Armageddon is linked to its predicted decline in the world scene owing to crime, subversion, and economic collapse. Others predict a coming dictatorship in America. Not all prophecy teaching is consistent in detail, but it all reflects a common mood.

There is always, though, emphasis that, however grim the future, it is an exciting time for the Christian. Lindsey, with his breezy style, his occasional references to agnostic professors, drugs, and occultism, makes the message "relevant" to the world of young people. Those who take the route of apocalyptic consciousness sense that the impending momentous events will be thrilling, like a technicolor movie. There will be the neo-Babylonian pomp of the great dictator, the hundreds of millions of uniforms and marching feet at dusty Armageddon, the atomic destruction of city after city. Those Christians taken out just before these events by the rapture will doubtless be able to watch it all from somewhere overhead like a mighty drama on a worldwide stage, just as before they had been in but not of this world. Since these observers know that in just a short time the Millennium will begin, they can combine compassionate sorrow at the temporary sufferings of the many with joyful expectations. They know that the sufferings are birthpangs, necessary to show the extreme of sin, but that in a matter of months, weeks, or days, they will be no longer.

BETHEL TABERNACLE

The radical apocalypticists (unlike traditional American apocalypticists like the Seventh-Day Adventists) tend to "drop out" of ordinary society to form tight communities like Lindsey's and to watch the signs of the times appear. But another wing of the movement, without denying the apocalyptic predictions, reintegrates young people into the stream of events. It is a method of resocialization of the lost, imposing upon them once again the "work ethic" with its deferred reward and orientation toward the accomplishment of tasks in this present world.

Interestingly, one of the best examples of this process is to be seen in a Pentecostal church, Bethel Tabernacle in Redondo Beach, California. The minister, the late Rev. Lyle Steenis, had a remarkably successful ministry with young people, although at first sight one might wonder why this is so. He was fifty-ish, heavy-set, with short hair and a clean-shaven face. When I attended his service, he wore a green suit with a white shirt and gold tie clasp. His grammar, accent, and rhetoric told me he was a country preacher from Appalachia, a man of more faith than formal education, with the timeless shrewdness and sincerity of his lineage. But if he had none of the externalia of the hip generation he communicated one thing: that he cares and that he can bring those who have strayed back into the world of his traditional American values and the intensity of his experience.

Coming from Pennsylvania, Steenis started this church shortly after the Second World War as an independent pentecostal mission. In 1968 a young man named Breck Stevens, on drugs and alienated from his family, was converted to Jesus by Steenis and began working with him. The preaching and evangelism of this man in his late teens brought scores of scruffy street people into the church. Inevitably protests arose from the established congregation. But Steenis adamantly supported Stevens. All but about twenty of the former congregation left. Now the church is packed with a different congregation twice on Sunday and several nights a week. They are, many of them, ex-dopers and runaways, wearing all sorts of styles of clothes and hair.[18]

On the Sunday I attended Bethel Tabernacle the service opened with old gospel hymns accompanied by a piano. Often individuals, moved by a song, raised one hand in dedication. The congregation stood for prayer, led by the pastor in a loud clear voice. The prayer included long petitions for servicemen and country. As he prayed for these and other intentions, there was a growing crescendo of "Amen" and "Yes, Lord," until an oceanic roar from the whole church undergirded the intense fiery words of the preacher.

Before the collection, Mr. Steenis spoke to the congregation. He said the work was supported by free will offerings from dedicated Christians; money was not wanted from guests. He told of the history of this church, now attracting nationwide attention. After the morning service, he said, they would go out on the beaches to bring in people for the evening services. The Lord's Supper, he said, is given once a month.

He told that the church emphasizes work, saving, giving 10 percent, and being responsible. He spoke of the "thirty-second drug cure"—accepting Christ. There were testimonies from a number of young people—"I'm happy," "Jesus is wonderful."

During the sermon, there were continual shouts of "Amen," or "That's right!" An elderly lady, like a prophetess, interrupted the preacher twice to stand up and give a discourse in "tongues." The preacher then and there halted his sermon to interpret the message. This procedure is characteristic of the pentecostal tradition.

The sermon emphasized Christian freedom—the Christian has gotten away from "rules and regulations." But the Christian doesn't need or want drugs or cigarettes. There is, he said, a "cigarette sack" by the altar of the church where packs and cartons are thrown in by converts. The Christian has a fuller, richer life with more color, based on the "full Bible"—the "Protestant churches" have taken the insides out of it.

He stressed that becoming a Christian means taking a responsible role in society. What the Bible says about the disciple taking no money with him doesn't apply today because conditions are different. Conversion means putting a scattered identity back together again; one rebuilt with real values, with respect for the military, for work and self-responsibility. The new Christian should get a job and live an ordered life. He should not feel he needs to give more than a tithe, 10 percent, to the church. It is part of his responsibility to save some of his money for the future so that he is not a burden on others.

At the end of the service some went up to kneel around the altar, with its open Bible, praying fervently and speaking quietly in "tongues." "Tongues," Steenis had said in the sermon, are a sign of rebirth—like the babbling of a babe.

ARTHUR BLESSITT

Another Jesus movement figure who has increasingly connected his ministry to current history is the Rev. Arthur Blessitt. Famous for his Sunset Strip work (described in the book *Turned on to Jesus*) in the days when it was a capital for runaways, Blessitt has more recently been traveling about the world, witnessing in newsworthy places.

On the Strip, he was a colorful figure. Claiming 10,000 converts as a result of his midnight services, his Christian street cheers, his titanic battles with night club owners and the Los Angeles County Sheriff's Department, the Southern Baptist Blessitt's central message was not apocalyptic, but simply conversion to Christ, giving up drugs, and returning home. He received his most publicity in 1969 when he chained himself for thirty days to a large cross on the street after he had been evicted from his center on the Strip because of pressure from night club owners, or so he claimed, and could find no building to rent. The demonstration—Blessit said the issue was, "Is there room for Jesus Christ on Sunset Strip?"—eventually produced new quarters.

However, by 1970 Sunset Strip was no longer where the action was. Blessitt moved on to a ministry in Times Square, New York, but soon left it to carry a large cross and preach at meetings on a march throughout England, Scotland, and Ireland. In Manchester over 15,000 marched behind him. In violence-torn Belfast, he claimed, both Catholics and Protestants joined in the march; he did his part to heal the deep religious feuds of that city.

Then, returning to his native land, Blessitt jumped into the 1972 presidential primary election in New Hampshire to organize his supporters to follow candidates around, demanding that they tell whether or not they were committed Christians. He called on the next president to "call a national day of repentance, prayer, fasting, and brotherhood beginning with his inauguration," and to "live his life and lead this nation on the teachings of the Bible." He sought 20,000 New Hampshire signatures on a statement demanding this commitment of candidates. But the flamboyant minister from Mississippi and the Sunset Strip sparked little fire in the Granite State.

Living in apocalyptic expectation, reintegrating the alienated into the values demanded by living in a deferred reward historical stream, demanding conversion of the places and persons who shape history—these are three ways in which a movement whose ultimate focus transcends history relates to it. This is to be expected, for the genius of the Judaeo-Christian tradition has been its acceptance of historical time as the arena of God's action.

6

Communes and the Children of God

COMMUNES AND APOCALYPTIC SECTS

JUST BEFORE THE TIME OF CHRIST, the Qumran community in ancient Palestine, which produced the famous Dead Sea Scrolls, withdrew into the desert and awaited the coming of a "Teacher of Righteousness" and a battle of the forces of light against those of darkness. From that day until now, apocalyptic groups have tended to form communal societies. A tight group, studying the Scriptures and confirming each other in eager interpretation, sustains the mood and effects the spread of apocalyptic ideas better than a parish church or individual commitment.

An institutional church, even if committed to an apocalyptic outlook like those of the Adventist denominations, acquires property and program involvements which absorb energy, presume a long future, and so dilute apocalyptic fervor. But the Christian communard, having left all to live in day-by-day expectancy, has wholly invested himself in a style which may reinforce apocalyptic hope and indeed may demand that it be fulfilled for validation of the commitment.

It is possible, of course, for Christian communes to be oriented toward values of stability and economic survival as well as reinforcement of faith. The Hutterian Brethren, for example, have lived a generally stable life in the U.S. and Canada since immigrating from Russia (where they had gone from Switzerland in the Reformation period) beginning in 1874. Numbering now about 13,000, they manage prosperous communal farms using modern equipment. But they wear plain dress, maintain a quiet traditional piety, and keep themselves separate, except for business matters, from their neighbors.

A more modern example is the Bruderhof movement, a set of communal farms in Latin America, England, and the U.S., founded by the German pacifist philosopher Eberhard Arnold in 1920. While they share many beliefs and observances with the Hutterites, they do not isolate themselves so much from the outside world. Other Christian communal groups could be cited, such as the Koinonia Community in Americus, Georgia, and Reba Place in Evanston, Illinois. Traditional Catholic and Orthodox monasticism is comparable, but has the additional "perfectionist" requirement of celibacy, as well as a different relation to the church as a whole.

These groups share with the new Jesus movement communes a belief that true Christianity requires a life of perfection, and that this is best found in the creation of a new society in which all members share the same conviction. In practice, however, the older groups do not now share the apocalyptic expectation of the Jesus movement communes. They see themselves instead as silent witnesses in the midst of a world which has much to learn and which they can teach even as they are sheltered from it for the sake of preserving fidelity to their Gospel. Strongly pacifist and pietistic, they are like islands in the midst of a violent, godless sea.

The Jesus movement communes are by contrast more like floating arks in a sea about to drown everything. The way of life is less stable, more improvised. Apocalyptic hope colors everything; they see no need to build a long-term economic or social base since they view their venture as temporary for the few years remaining before the end. Like the early Franciscans, they are prepared to be flying squads of missionaries into the world, and to change their bases and structures frequently. They are more dependent on charismatic leadership. They have the characteristics of a movement just coalescing and which as yet has felt little need to care for the future. Unlike the Hutterites, all present adult members are joiners rather than people brought up in the commune; they are people who have had to undergo intense personality reorientation to adjust to communal life, and they have the fervor and problems of converts.

These Christian communes new and old bear the sociological characteristics of the "sect," such as withdrawal from society, emphasis upon conversion as a condition of membership, voluntary joining, austerity of life, and an implied or explicit condemnation of society outside the group. But while the sect may expect a conversion experience of an appropriate sort as a condition of joining (unlike the cult, which characteristically centers around mystical, expansion-of-consciousness experience as a continuing incentive and goal), it is mainly concerned with a hard, more or less legalistic, living out the life to which its members are called. Once there has been the initial experience of glory, then comes the grimmer, but also satisfying, task of showing real perseverence in commitment by living it day in and day out and witnessing to it. Obviously, a community of similarly-minded believers is an aid to both the initial and long pull experiences. The withdrawal and deferred reward seriousness in intent to follow the Bible (or other authority) in every detail combine to make the withdrawn communal sect a potential hotbed of perfectionist and/or apocalyptic thought—and persons of that bent will in turn be drawn to the commune.

However, older "established" sects with a well-honed routine will be likely to emphasize perfectionism more than apocalypticism. Withdrawal becomes habitual, passed on from generation to generation, and the conversion requirement becomes nominal. At first, as though in reflection of the converts' own intense, radical rejection of the world as it is, apocalyptic expectation will typically permeate the sectarian's life. Years later, that hope may be difficult to sustain, and he may find himself in practice more and more concerned to show by the perfectionism of his belief and behavior only his separation from a "world" which seems in no hurry to pass away.

Most of the Jesus movement outside of the communes is still too fluid, too much just a social movement to be called a sect, although obviously it has many sectarian characteristics, as do many of the churches it centers upon. But it also has cultic characteristics carried over from the new consciousness of the late sixties and focusing on ecstatic experience. As the movement rationalizes itself, it will undoubtedly take more and more its logical sectarian shape, insofar as it does not simply become assimilated into routinized Christianity, evangelical or otherwise. This process is illustrated in the communes and their likely ultimate end we see in groups like the Amish and Hutterites, communal or quasi communal withdrawal sects.

Almost all of the Jesus movement communes are apocalyptic, even more than the rank and file of the movement. Mansion Messiah, as we have seen, discusses prophecy and apocalyptic timetables avidly. But at its home church, Calvary Chapel, the apocalyptic sense is more characteristic of the leadership than the ordinary youthful attenders. For most of the latter, one gathers, present mystical identity with Jesus, the "saved" feeling, and practical ventures such as the record "Love Song" are of more interest. Intense apocalypticism and separatist, communal life styles go hand in hand.

Of course, Jesus movement communes have other motifs too. They do provide for sustaining mutual ecstasy here and now. In 1970 I visited a now abandoned Christian commune called the House of Emmanuel. Located near Sumas, Washington, only a few miles from the Canadian border, it was a tiny bungalow supplemented by a big army tent on a steep gravel mountain road in lush grass and a stately evergreen forest. Snowcapped peaks buttressed the horizon; the air was scented and tangy, as intoxicating as wine.

But despite the glory of the setting, my initial impression of the commune was that of depressing squalor. Some fifty boys, girls, and ragged children were living together in obvious poverty. The plumbing was a single pump and a single outdoor privy. Water for cooking, washing, and bathing was heated over open fires. The kitchen, with its old-fashioned wood-burning stove, its scavenged food, its chipped dishes and grime, suggested a melancholy frowziness and privation which overshadowed any warm sense of the pioneer past.

The old-time note was a bit more positive in the spare ornamentation. No reading matter was apparent on the ancient tables of the living room except the King James Bible. On the walls were quaint nineteenth-century lithographs of Jesus and Bible scenes. Incongruously, the Sacred Heart and the Christ in the Garden of popular Catholic and Protestant piety, respectively, hung side by side.

But the twentieth century, not the nineteenth, was the background of these young people. They said they had been through the "hippie scene"—wandering, drugs, occultism—and by chance, or grace, had found Christ and come together in Seattle. They had an ancient bus to go into cities for evangelistic work. Their smiling enthusiasm transcended the surrounding grubbiness. "Praise the Lord" and "God loves you" were continually on their lips; together with Bible verses these lines were greeting, farewell, and answer to all problems. They related that they frequently gathered for deep prayer meetings, lasting several hours, in the lantern-lit army tent.

A shared mood and emotional response, passed by suggestion and example from one person to another, intensified by singing and the prayer meetings, sustained group life. Like Mansion Messiah, this was largely a "temporary" commune rather than a permanent vocation. Veterans of the dropout life, on their way to rehabilitation through Jesus, might stay there six months to a year. I was struck by both the intensity and simplicity of the commune's spiritual life and left wondering how appalling the life out of which they came must have been to make this material crudity and spiritual absolutism seem preferable, even for a short while.

THE CHILDREN OF GOD

One of the most prominent communal groups is the Children of God. Fervently apocalyptic, strong believers that this is the last generation and that they are the chosen witnesses called out for these final days, they are well known to TV watchers and newspaper readers. They were present at such landmark events of a tumultuous era as the Manson trial, the trial of the "Chicago Seven," and Senator Dirksen's lying-in-state at the capitol. On these occasions the Children dressed in sackcloth, wore yokes about their necks, bore large placards on their chests presenting words of Scripture about judgment and repentance of nations, and carried great staves which beat with a heavy, ominous rhythm as they marched. They walked or stood in meaningful silence, an ancient testimony to a modern nation in mortal danger of the wrath to come.

Behind this prophetic public stance is a communal life shared by several thousand young people. They are dedicated only to the work of the gospel, an extreme Biblical literalism, an authoritarian organization, and intense apocalypticism. Around them swirl extensive controversy, countless tearful battles between parents and sons or daughters, and much talk of deliverance out of the world of drugs and counter culture. The Children's life is one of seeming exuberant joy but no privacy, virtually no reading except the Bible and lessons on it, and educational techniques that have been compared to brainwashing. In short, it seems a simultaneous combination of Qumran, an Israeli kibbutz, and a coeducational monastic order.

This is how a tract of the Children puts their calling.

> THE PROPHETS OF DOOM OF THE "CHILDREN OF GOD" IN DRAMATIC DEMONSTRATIONS ACROSS THE NATION ARE WARNING OF THE DEATH OF THE NATION IN THE RED SACKCLOTH OF MOURNING, THE YOKE OF BONDAGE & THE ROD OF JUDGMENT & BEARING THE SCROLLS OF PROPHECY. IN THUNDERING SILENCE THEY HAVE STOOD IN VIGIL BETWEEN THE VIOLENCE OF REVOLUTION & SINS OF THE SYSTEM FROM WHITE HOUSE TO CAPITOL, U N TO CATHEDRAL & FROM COAST TO COAST! ON NATIONAL TV AND FRONT-PAGE HEADLINES THESE MOD-

ERN PROPHETS HAVE CONDEMNED THE NATION FOR ITS INIQUITIE$, INEQUITIE$, BLOOD$HED, & OPPRE$$ION, $ELFRIGHTEOU$NE$$ & HYPOCRI$Y & RIDICULOU$ RELIGION$! THESE MILITANT ADVOCATES OF *SPIRITUAL REVOLUTION* AS THE *ONLY SOLUTION* IN THIS *LAST GENERATION* ARE CRUSADING FOR A RETURN TO PRIMITIVE FAITH AND THE SIMPLE LIFE OF THE PATRIARCHS IN THE PEACE-FULL, UNPOLLUTED, UNSELFISH ATMOSPHERE OF TRUTH & LOVE AS TOLD BY JESUS! THESE SPIRITUAL REVOLUTIONARIES ARE ESTABLISHING COMMUNES OF TRUTH, PEACE & LOVE ACROSS THE NATION OPEN TO THOSE WHO WANT TO HELP OTHERS.

It will be noted that this tract, aimed chiefly at the street people who are the primary source of recruitment to the Children, holds up counter culture ideals and attacks impartially the sins of revolutionaries and those of the "Establishment." In talking with the Children, one can hear lurid talk of Communist persecutions of Christians. They also honored Senator Dirksen's funeral because of his advocacy of prayer in public schools. Yet they are equally condemnatory of the materialism of their capitalistic families.

The Children of God see themselves as a remnant in the midst of a world already too far gone for secular salvation, about to tear itself apart in its final death throes through meaningless struggles between different kinds of faithlessness. They have taken themselves out to escape the worst of the Tribulation, and to call others who will hear to come out with them. They alone are the true church, for they alone are uncompromised and follow the Bible literally, even to the verse, chanted over and over, about having all things in common. They are the pure early church come back, fittingly, to share in the last days and the Return of the King.

The economics of the Children are communal. No member of the order has an outside job. They receive money, of course, from people who join; some bring much and some little. Each member has a trade practiced within the organization: mechanic, seamstress, cook. They do not need much cash, for they get leftover food from shops and warehouses, or grow their own in country centers. Members are kept on short leash, having little occasion to spend and nothing to spend of their own.

In 1971, the Children of God had some 2,500 to 3,000 members in about thirty colonies throughout North America and Europe. At the time I visited the colony at 5th and Towne streets in the Los Angeles skid row section, it housed some 120 members. The Children were later evicted from that old mission owned by evangelist Fred Jordan, but that is another story.

As I approached the building one evening, I found no sign outside indicating the presence of the Children and the door was locked. Given the neighborhood, the lock was perhaps understandable. Ringing the bell with some apprehension, I was greeted with "God loves you" and ushered into a reception room. The room held four or five young people. One girl was behind a desk; the others were seated on a bench studying the Bible, repeating verses over and over to memorize them. One boy was speaking, a little dissociatedly I thought, about coming earthquakes. Before I could be admitted further into the building, the receptionist had to make some phone calls. Eventually a young lady named Faith, whom I later learned is a daughter of the founder of the movement and one of its principal leaders, appeared to talk with me. In an intelligent and reassuring way, she answered my questions. She told me they are absolute fundamentalists, that they believe this is the last generation, and that they will experience persecution, even as Christians do now in Russia. They believe communal life is a scriptural necessity.

The Children are against the churches, as well as against the "Jesus movement" of the press for just seeking "highs." She said they do not fight in wars, but do register for the draft. I commented that in some ways they sounded like the early Quakers. Faith liked the comparison; she said there needs to be a renewal of the Church in every generation. In one generation it was the Reformation, in another the early Quaker movement, in ours it is the Children. Each generation, she said, needs a group that "drops out *all the way,*" with no compromise. Unlike the "Jesus people," she added, the Children are building a new communal society, a new civilization, the Kingdom of God. They are also the Saints in the Book of Life who, according to Revelation, will go through the tribulation before the Last Day.

Again like the early Quakers, the Children have no "formal" worship. They study the Bible in the morning, and go out "as God leads" in the afternoon to evangelize. They round up street people from parks, beaches, boulevards, and bring them back as guests for dinner. During these activities, worship may begin "spontaneously." They do recognize the formal sacraments; they may have baptisms in the ocean, or Communion with bread or "anything, anytime, as the Lord leads."

Faith invited me to stay for supper with the Children. The dining hall was packed with people dressed in jeans, maxis, T-shirts, sandals, or boots—anything except shorts or short skirts on girls—and hair of all styles and lengths. All wore tiny yoke symbols on cords around their necks, but I was told they never wear crosses because that symbol, as an ornament, is too much connected with "hypocrisy."

A sprinkling of guests was present too. The tables were laden with plain but very adequate food. However, as we sat down, someone began a song on a guitar, and the whole room started singing. It mattered not that the food was getting cold; the Spirit was upon the assembly. Songs included "You got to be a Babe!" and "Revolution—All Power to the People of God!" the last a chant accompanied by the gesture of a fist and a three-finger sign. After each song, they raised hands and spoke praises, often moving easily into glossalalia.

There were testimonies: new members praised unqualifiedly the experiences they had had with the Children. Positive statements were presented by the visitors. One boy said uneasily he was AWOL from the military, but had felt the Lord was calling him to seek out the Children. He received many cheers. The mood was happy euphoria, sustained by a very limited range of verbal expression. Little was said beyond discussion of the necessities of life and support of one another's faith with ecstatic "Praise the Lord" and Bible verses.

I sensed what the reality of the group is: the Children of God as a way of life breaks down individualizing personality structures as thoroughly as possible. Those are of "the natural man." The group destroys ordinary subjectivity by leaving a person no time for self-communing; it even endeavors to destroy the vocabulary used in subjectivity by replacing it with biblical language. There is no privacy.

A new member—a "babe"—is expected to have a rebirth experience. He must confess his sins and be born again of the Spirit. He signifies this by taking a new name—the Children are all called by biblical names: Jethro, Mark, Jeremiah, Deborah, Faith. The "babe" must learn the rules—no drugs, alcohol, tobacco; no raiding the refrigerator; no time to oneself; no possessions. His incoming and outgoing mail will be censored. He has a "buddy" who accompanies him at all times, even to the toilet. He is kept busy from morning to night. He has relatively little sleep and does not eat until noon. He is given a pocket Bible and a lesson book which gives the only authorized interpretation of the Bible. He studies these constantly; he has to memorize many verses a day. His mornings will be spent in Bible classes reciting verses while they may be pounded into his ears electronically by headphones. The dropout rate, I was told, is about 15 percent, mostly in the first few weeks.

We must remember that a very high percentage of these "babes" have previously been drug addicts, prostitutes, and the like. The intense training can be compared to boot camp in the military, or to a novitiate in an austere monastic order. It is a strenuous experience designed to mold a new personality in a short period, using every trick of fatigue, strain, loud repetition, and authoritarianism to shatter one psychic structure and substitute for it the values and vocabulary of another.

After a time as a "babe," the new member becomes a Younger Brother, and finally an Elder Brother. He is also called a Disciple. He must learn a trade useful to the Children; leathercraft, art, photography, agriculture, etc. But he will not take an outside job and will never return to the "world" except to witness.

Like the primitive church, the Children are led by persons called Apostles, Elders, and Deacons. These are, it is said, neither elected nor appointed, but "God-consulted." The Disciples pray about a vacant position and are given a name. It is said that decisions are made by the Elders in the same way—in council by prayerful group consensus.

Witnessing, or "sharing," follows a fairly set pattern. A busload of Children will invade a likely street or park and strike up one of their bouncy, irresistible songs. They may well accompany some songs with charming dances, for dancing is held not to be sinful, since David danced before the Ark of the Covenant. Most of the Children's dances are based on Jewish folk dance, for the Children emphasize the Jewish heritage of Christianity, as well as modern Israel; some aspects of the communal life are modeled on the kibbutz. After a crowd has gathered, they intersperse singing and dancing with brief words of prophetic warning and testimonies. Then they break up to talk individually with onlookers, expounding the Scriptures.

Unless you know the Bible very well, as few people do these days, you will not come away victorious from such an encounter. If a prospective convert puts up undue resistance, Children have been known to "smite" him by striking him with the Bible! Those whom they can persuade they will bring home to dinner, and some will not see the outside world again except as one of the Children. The silent public vigils are held only occasionally.

Each colony of the Children is under the supervision of an Elder. Each is financially independent and seems to have some variation in schedule and perhaps style. But they like to keep in close touch by ham radio and video tape, as well as by letters and "in-house" papers. Typically, a house will have separate floors for men, women, and married couples. A few couples have joined, including a retired Navy commander and his wife, a motherly woman who heads the sewing room in one colony. Many are married within the order—not from love-matches, for dating and courtship are forbidden, but by selection by the Elders. The Children of God want lots of babies born within the household.

Because mistrust of the "system" extends to its medicine as well as its other devices, women do not have the benefit of a doctor to assist them at a birth. Nor is there any privacy. A mother gives birth surrounded by the other women of the commune who support her with prayer.

Education in the "system" is trusted no more than its medicine. Children are educated in the Children of God's own schools, which employ Montessori methods. As on the kibbutzes of Israel, children are taken from their parents at three to live with others of their age group; they are permitted only a few hours a week with their parents. The children are called Benjaminites, or for fun BBB's—"Benjamin Bottle Breakers." An issue of the COG newspaper gives a strange and disturbing account of a visit of fifteen BBB's, ages two to nine, to a zoo. They tried to teach the mynah bird to say "Praise the Lord" and some Bible verses. When he proved reprobate, a chaperone "blasted" him, saying, "Whosoever turneth away his ear from hearing the law, even his prayer shall be an abomination." At the lion's cage they gave the "Lion of Judah yell." Then they gathered around an evolution exhibit to sing "My Father's Not a Monkey," and left about fifty broken bottles there.

The accounts of converts to the Children are as endlessly varied as any 2000 human odysseys. One young man tells of leaving home at sixteen, entering the "hippie" life, thinking LSD was the highest "high" possible, and becoming a drug dealer. He was quickly very well off materially. Then his wife left him, and he was "busted." Hearing about the COG, he visited them in his time of trouble. He was converted, but went to court sustained by their prayers and then to jail to serve his sentence and enter the order with a clean record. Another member was a campus radical who suddenly and inexplicably found his whole value system turned upside down when he heard the Children on a campus visit. Others were intensely religious young people, in orthodox churches or in the movement, who could not resist the greater apparent commitment of the Children.

THE STORY OF THE CHILDREN

The Children of God was started in the late 1960s by the Rev. David Berg. Mr. Berg, an ordained minister and nondenominational evangelist now in his fifties, had ministered in a church in Arizona. His departure from this church involved some sort of unpleasantness. He moved to California to work as a public relations agent for the Rev. Fred Jordan, a pentecostal minister who had established the American Soul Clinic in 1944. That work had become a large operation, including a skid row mission in Los Angeles, orphanages in Korea and Hong Kong, and rural property in California and Texas used as training centers and rest camps for missionaries. These projects were financed by contributions received by Jordan's popular radio and TV program, "Church in the Home." However, Berg was not able to work congenially with Jordan and moved to Huntington Beach, where his mother (also a radio evangelist) lived. Here he took over a Teen Challenge post, renamed it the Light Club, and attracted a small group of young followers in late 1967 or early 1968.

Here it was that the Children of God actually began. An intense, close-knit body met with Berg for Bible classes and decided to try Christian communal living under his leadership. The present real rulers of the Children of God, including Berg's own children, two boys and two girls now in their twenties and married, derive from the community of this period. Berg insisted that his followers drop out of their jobs.

About a year later Berg received by supernatural means information that California was threatened by an earthquake and that he and his group should leave. Numbering now about fifty, they left for eight months of wandering through the Southwest. This era has now, in the lore of the Children, acquired a quasi-mythological status roughly equivalent to that of the Exodus of the Jews from Egypt or the "Long March" of the Chinese Communists. It is related that at times they were reduced to eating grass, and that during the epic journey they first became known to themselves as the Children of God.

They consciously compared their history to that of the Children of Israel and some of their own personalities with the great figures of the Bible who had become so familiar to them through assiduous study. Certainly this period, like similar periods in the histories of other religious groups, established a demarcating sense of group identity, mythos, and cohesion. They testified wherever they went, continuing a practice (characteristic of the Huntington Beach days too, but now abandoned) of entering "straight" churches en masse on Sunday morning, full of "Amens" and "Praise the Lords," much to the consternation of the regular parishioners.

The Children had grown to over a hundred when, early in 1970, the wandering ended thanks to the help of Fred Jordan. He offered the Children the use of his skid row mission, and also a 400-acre ranch in Texas. A little later a date and citrus ranch near Coachella, California, was added. The Children settled down and prospered. The details of the regimen were worked out. They began the famous vigils; they sent out groups to establish colonies in other cities around the country. As a result of much media publicity, including a sympathetic nationwide TV special early in 1971, their numbers grew daily. David Berg did not live in a colony but withdrew from active day-to-day supervision of the order; this he turned over to his children and lieutenants.

Enroth, Ericson, and Peters argue intriguingly that both the Children and Jordan were trying to use each other. Jordan had them appear regularly on his programs. The sight of these former "hippies" and "dopers" with their youthful faces testifying to what the power of Jesus had done for them, and sometimes having their long hair cut on TV, warmed the hearts of many a "Middle American" viewer and produced vast contributions—some have estimated as much as half a million dollars—within a year for his youth work. For the Children, the nonworking beneficiaries of at least some of this income, the period was an opportunity to stabilize their life.[19]

But the alliance of conservative, Establishment-oriented preacher and the Children of God was too unstable to last. Word spread among Jordan's public that the Children were not just clean-cut young Christians, but as virulently against ordinary churches and the "system" as any leftist radical. In August, 1971, a Parents Committee to Free Our Sons and Daughters from the Children of God organized in San Diego and put pressure on Jordan. They claimed that converts were held by the Children through hypnotism, drugs, and brainwashing techniques. In late 1971 Jordan discovered that the Children were "teaching hate" and were too tenacious in retaining membership. He asked them to leave his three properties.

The open break occurred when Jordan asked that the leader of the Coachella colony, Beltshazzar, called Belt for short, be replaced. Belt had questioned why the Children were allowed to use only ten acres of the property and not an additional hundred acres bought with money donated on behalf of the youth work. Although Jordan indicated the Children could stay with new leadership, they all sided with Belt and evacuated the ranch and all other Jordan properties, leaving behind $40,000 worth of improvements at Coachella alone, rather than accept direction from Jordan regarding their affairs.

The fracas received considerable coverage in the southern California press and TV. The Children settled for a few days in Los Angeles, MacArthur Park, where they sang, danced, and evangelized, often in front of cameras. A running battle continued with Jordan over possessions left in the skid row mission building: he locked them out and refused to let them retrieve their meagre effects until a new bus they held, which he said he had loaned them but which belonged to him, was returned.

In a few days the Children all moved to San Diego into a slum house. Around the end of 1971, alleging both an atmosphere of persecution and the immanence of cataclysmic earthquakes in California, they left that state entirely. The California children mostly went to the Pacific Northwest, which became, for the time being, the center of the movement. Here the Children were greatly strengthened by the acquisition of two major Jesus movement leaders, together with parts of the followings of each: Linda Meissner in Seattle and Russ Griggs in Vancouver. Both joined the Children only a few days before the expulsion from Fred Jordan's property. In addition, David Hoyt, a movement leader in Atlanta, joined the Children and moved to the Northwest.

The move hardly ended the publicity and controversy surrounding the Children. Shortly after the transfer to the Northwest, the *Seattle Post-Intelligencer* came by several confidential letters written by David Berg (called "Moses") to COG leaders or, in some cases, to "all but babes." It appeared that Berg, from an unknown location, had been guiding the organization as a sort of hidden eminence through correspondence called "Mo-letters." Several of these were in a box accidentally thrown in with the belongings of an exmember who moved out. She gave them to a friend in drug therapy work, who passed them on to the newspaper. The paper quoted from them extensively in an excellent and balanced series of articles about the organization.

The published "Mo-letters" offer blunt, critical advice on day-to-day problems, often suggesting a more pragmatic course than one might have supposed from the COG's uncompromising public line. Regarding Linda Meissner, Berg says "for God's sake" let her continue her speaking engagements and "give her something to do, even though she blasts herself away." He suggests common sense in the handling of the merger of Linda's "Jesus People Army" with the Children, and in the management of property belonging to Griggs's and Hoyt's previous works. The COG leaders should not push too hard to change organizational names and titles—let Meissner, Griggs, and their followers "feel good" by continuing their old labels and serving on the board.

Apparently reversing a previous policy, Berg also suggests the Children let the government support members as much as possible through welfare and other programs. He advises the COG not get in the position of owning property—they need to be free to move at any time, and property only leads to entanglement. He harps considerably on the break with Jordan, predicting that God will cast out the television preacher as Jordan cast out the Children of God. He calls Jordan "King Saul," whom of course David bested in the Bible. Berg continually assimilates events in the history of the Children of God with biblical stories, with himself, as Moses or David, in a leading role. Interspersed with the practical advice and the biblical identifications are reports of visions and divine communications, of his own and his late mother's. For example, he once says that "the great archangel Michael" has become the special guardian angel of the Children of God.

What has raised most eyebrows, though, is "A Shepherd-Time Story," a simply written allegory found in one of the letters. Berg said the Lord showed it to him "in pictures, like a movie." The story was dedicated to all the Children, especially the Benjamin Bottle Breakers. It speaks of true and false shepherds, good and bad sheepfolds, robbers, wolves, and "a great big Jesus with a big stick" who "clobbers the wolves." It says the "folds of David"—a play on Berg's first name—are the happiest of all. It portrays the tenderness and beauty of the "shepherdesses" in this fold, and the delights which everyone in this fold enjoy. Included among pleasures like laughing, singing, dancing, and playing was a four-letter word for sexual intercourse; and Berg added that many little lambs are born.[20]

Leaders of the Children in Seattle verified the authenticity of all the letters, and were understandably defensive about the implications of the "Shepherd-Time Story." They claimed that "Moses" uses a special language which those outside do not fully understand, that he must use the argot of the street people with whom they work, and that no sexual activity or bearing of lambs takes place outside of marriage among the Children. The letter did not necessarily imply otherwise. But the vulgar language and sensual imagery stands in strange contrast to the ultrafundamentalist face they present to the world. Yet such pastoral delights fit the concrete vision of the Millenium, or of the New Heaven and Earth, which the apocalypticist, in contrast to the mystic, generally has, and which he believes his community in some sense anticipates, even as it awaits its unveiling.

The Children of God have continued to be controversial. Spearheaded by the Parents' Committee, opponents claimed that drugs, hypnosis, and kidnapping have been involved in recruitment. Young people who have left the order have, as one might expect, brought back grim accounts. They have said that some Children, exhausted by the regimen, have had untreated colds and even hepatitis, that their time in the community was like a dazed, unreflecting dream, a peculiar psychic state that only "broke" when they managed to leave, sometimes by being taken out by enraged relatives. They have claimed that leaders eat steak while ordinary Disciples and Babes must subsist on tainted meat. They have also reported the leaders are stockpiling rifles, and that they talk in a strange agitated way, combined with an unnerving direct stare. However, other parents, and some visiting newsmen and ministers, have been favorably impressed with the Children's community. They have commented on the atmosphere of love, and the success the order has had with drug problems.

The Children have countered the Parents' Committee's charges with a $1,100,000 suit for libel and slander against its four leaders. In addition, they argue that some of the same parents who accuse them of "kidnapping" have tried to take their children forcibly, against the young person's will, from the community—which they say amounts to the same thing. The COG does not take people under eighteen without the parents' consent—some parents, often religiously motivated, have gladly given such consent. The Children contend that other parents are seemingly unconcerned about their offspring overindulging in drugs, or sex, leading a meaningless materialistic life, or else are so preoccupied with their own affairs that they are unaware of the problems of their children in these respects. Yet when the same children finally turn in despair to membership in the Children of God, they protest vehemently, as though being a radical Christian was worse than being a "doper" or going to jail—as though religious fanaticism were the worst offense of all.

Finally, there is no way the Children of God can be evaluated except on religious grounds. It makes no sense except in terms of a religious world view—which is the whole point. It is an apocalyptic community of "dropouts," motivated by a vision beyond the structures of this ordinary world. Like mysterious tantric communities of India and Tibet, it offers an intense short path to radical reversal of ordinary reality through destruction of common subjectivity, obedience, chanting of sacred verses, visions, and some kind of sacred use of sexual evocation. In addition to this, it has the Christian apocalyptic concern—it sees the Children of God as the messianic community, waiting in the hills for the tribulation and the creation of the new paradise. It sees itself reliving the dramas of the Bible. If all this is true, the Children of God are beyond judgment by those attached to the present world which to them is crumbling and passing away. It if is false, they are fools—unless even misguided belief makes life more interesting than doubt and cynicism, and even erroneous commitment is a deeper joy than ambiguous realism.

7

On the Campus

THE JESUS MOVEMENT DID NOT BEGIN ON THE CAMPUS, but it caught on there almost immediately. In some places it virtually took the proportions of another campus craze, as psychedelica had before it. Indeed, it is intriguing to reflect how many American cultural movements have their ultimate roots in drug-taking circles, or like the Jesus movement are a direct reaction against them. The externals of a "drug culture" have more than once spread from out of a tiny, alienated group in which drug-taking played an important role in providing motifs for the posters, literature, music, dress, and language of the campuses and, via them, the general public. And the public, even though it formally disapproves of taking drugs, seems somehow infatuated with the products of the drug-altered mind. America has long had a fascination for the music, art, culture, and states of mind which come from hallucinogenic drugs or which counterfeit them. Before hippie-dom there was jazz, before that American fanciers of the opium-eating British and French "decadents."

The opening wedge and main vehicle of cultural assimilation for the Jesus movement on the campus has been evangelical groups independent of denominational ties. The two major ones are Campus Crusade for Christ and Inter-Varsity Christian Fellowship. These two groups have a solid evangelical tradition, and their very freedom from the denominational church has been an asset to them in attracting today's student population. Their campus appeal is the envy of most denominational programs. They have a very special place in the religious history of America and the British Commonwealth.

THE INTER-VARSITY CHRISTIAN FELLOWSHIP

The most venerable of these groups is Inter-Varsity Christian Fellowship. In the U.S. it goes back to the school year 1939-40, though it existed before that in Canada and England. It was started in England in the early twenties as an intercollegiate Christian union at Oxford and Cambridge. Then, as always, its work has depended on student initiative. Behind the student groups is an administrative and field staff of about one hundred people. Field staff personnel travel to campuses in their areas to work as "coaches" with student Bible discussion groups. The basic goal is evangelism and mission support. In December of 1970, Inter-Varsity conducted a missionary convention at the University of Illinois which drew 12,000, perhaps the largest student religious gathering in American history to that date.

More than other independent groups, Inter-Varsity stresses intellectual and social concerns. Emphasizing that for effective evangelism inward growth is necessary, it tries to strengthen the individual's spiritual and intellectual life. While the theological outlook is conservative and evangelical, Inter-Varsity does not get overattached to fundamentalist shibboleths, and also talks about Christian responsibility in society. It tries to help students function as Christians in their own environment, and to use its vocabulary, not that of a professional evangelist.

The group's methods vary according to situation, but will generally include Bible study groups, prayer groups, and weekend conferences, but no regular church services as such. According to an Inter-Varsity field worker interviewed in 1971, exact statistics are not kept on participation in these activities, but it was definitely up. He attributed the growth to "spin-off" from the Jesus movement. More entering freshmen than before, in the fall of 1971, were open to being identified as "Christians," whatever they may have meant by it.

The same worker saw changes in the style of expression of Christianity too. In the 50s and 60s, Inter-Varsity leaders tried to get away from ditty-like gospel songs toward hymns which were also great music. Now, with the advent of the guitar in virtually all youth worship, the trend is back to songs with bouncy tunes, usually in the words of Scripture, like "One in the Spirit." There is also more informality. The traditional campus approach—bringing in a "name" speaker—works less well than having a group with much student discussion and sharing. The emphasis is now on developing "action groups," small, tight student groups—almost cell groups—which study the Bible, pray, and work together to spread the name of Christ on a campus.

In the 70s, I was told, Inter-Varsity is experiencing more additions by real conversion than before. The membership covers a wider spectrum —the core is no longer necessarily just young people from conservative churches. Many have come by way of the drug and radical life style route. Occasionally there is tension in the groups between the prodigal and the son who was always faithful, and never journeyed to the psychedelic "far country," but "where there is life, there can be unity."

Inter-Varsity took hold in the days of the postwar religion boom, which was far more closely related to participation in the institutional church than the present movement. Inter-Varsity claims to be committed "to church, but not to a church." While it provides an experience of fellowship for today's subjectivity and experience-oriented young people, its leaders insist that, by itself, Inter-Varsity is not enough.

Inter-Varsity presents what might be called an intellectual's evangelicalism. The Bible discussions, "dig-ins," as they may be called, on particular verses and chapters, involve neither critical-historical explanation nor fundamentalist "proof-texting." Rather, the exact meaning, the personal-life implications, the intra-scriptural play of ideas and themes, are what is brought out in reverent, enthusiastic tones.

CAMPUS CRUSADE FOR CHRIST

The other major nondenominational group, Campus Crusade for Christ, presents a somewhat more aggressive, and inevitably less intellectual, image. It was founded in 1951 on the UCLA campus by Bill Bright, a former businessman, who is its present leader. In its literature and rhetoric, the teachings of Scripture present a clear-cut schema for salvation. The type of person attracted, or at least idealized in the literature, is a clean-cut, athletic kind of young American, interested in sports and likely to go into business after he graduates.

Campus Crusade has apparently been more successful than Inter-Varsity in attracting money and members. Its 1972 budget was $12 million; there were 3,000 full-time staff members working on 450 campuses. Each staffer is supposed to raise his own support by speaking to church and other groups about the work of CCC. Each receives an identical salary. One-fourth of the staff have ministry or graduate degrees; the others are strictly laymen with B.A.'s. Their training has been received in summer sessions, usually at the beautiful Crusade headquarters in a former hotel near Lake Arrowhead, California.

The Campus Crusade approach tends strongly toward a set formula. Literature and talks by Crusaders to general audiences usually begin with a statement of man's spiritual need. There will then be a proof of biblical accuracy based on prophecy fulfillment. Next comes the crux of the presentation: the "Four Spiritual Laws" formulated by Bill Bright. These, illustrated by Scriptural verses and simple diagrams, are

1. God *loves* you, and has a wonderful *plan* for your life.
2. Man is *sinful* and *separated* from God, thus he cannot know and experience God's love and plan for his life.
3. Jesus Christ is God's *only* provision for man's sin. Through him you can know and experience God's love and plan for your life.
4. We must individually *receive* Jesus Christ as Savior and Lord; then we can know and experience God's love and plan for our lives.

These laws, and similar simple evangelical truths, are circulated on campuses in a variety of ways. The basic organized activity is the Bible class, often held at noon or in the evening, if possible in large university rooms. A vast amount of literature, always beautifully printed, is distributed at meetings, on tables on campus and person-to-person. It will range in format from tiny pocket tracts to slick magazines to imitations of underground newspapers. But the message is always the same: Jesus Christ as understood in light of the Four Spiritual Laws.

Crusaders emphasize the dictum that no solution can be found to the world's problems—war, pollution, poverty—except as individuals accept Christ and then work to solve them. Radical and revolutionary tactics are definitely not the solution, any more than any other answer than Christ can care of an individual's sense of meaninglessness.

Crusade workers spend a large part of their time talking on the campus in this vein—to individuals, to groups such as fraternities and sororities. Sometimes a crowd will be gathered on the lawn or in an auditorium by special programs. On my campus these have included a weight-lifting demonstration by a Christian professional athlete and a demonstration of stage magic by an "illusionist," including a replication of the "calling up of the dead" by Spiritualist mediums. Both ended with testimony and "talking about Christ" by the performers, who were sponsored by the Crusade organization. Literature is also passed out on these occasions.

Campus Crusade has a special affinity for athletes. An allied organization is American Athletes in Action. The testimonial stories of Christian athletes are often given prominent place in the literature; it is presumed that they still are heroes and pacesetters for a great number of young people.

In June of 1972, Campus Crusade held a week-long evangelical gathering of young people in the Cotton Bowl stadium in Dallas called Explo '72. About 75,000 showed up. It was a big event for the Jesus movement, and probably the largest "camp meeting" ever to take place. Most in attendance were high school and college students. During the day they attended evangelism classes in churches and hotels; at night they met in the stadium to hear Jesus rock, shout Jesus yells like "Two bits, four bits, six bits, a dollar. All for Jesus stand up and holler," and make the One Way sign. It ended on Saturday with an eight-hour Jesus rock festival. The close ties of Campus Crusade with big-name evangelists was evidenced by the fact that the Honorary Chairman was Billy Graham, who called it a "religious Woodstock."

Conversions to Christ through Campus Crusade tend to fall into the basic evangelical pattern. One student said:

> I wanted to be different, but I didn't know how. I transferred to a college away from home and had a lot of freedom. I lived in a coed dormitory which had few restrictions, so it was that I started doing everything I felt like doing whenever I felt like doing it.
>
> But my mind went back to a text in the Bible, "Therefore if any man is in Christ, he is a new creature; the old things passed away; behold new things have come."
>
> It was hard to sleep at night. I had no peace. Relaxing was difficult. I was even afraid of the dark, because I knew that I was going against God and pretty soon something had to give.
>
> But after meeting some Christians on campus talking about Jesus, I realized that Jesus Christ has the power to give me power to do the things I want to do. I have stopped smoking and abusing sex, because I simply do not need to do these things anymore. I can even sleep now.

This account by a Crusader indicates its basis in the evangelical psychology. There is a psyche, like St. Augustine's, torn by the guilt which its very freedom arouses, seeking for an anchor positive enough to turn it in another direction. Sometimes the confrontational approach is what is necessary to raise the level of psychological energy enough to effect a change of course. Another Crusader said, "I can see how people could say that Crusaders try to button-hole people and get them against the wall and lecture. We just have something fantastic to share. So that's what we do."

In Campus Crusade there is an air of optimism about the future rare in church circles today. Some of this, of course, is the typical evangelical church preoccupation with producing success statistics and self-identification with a winning army—an identification suggested both by its name and by its liking for successful athletes and businessmen.

But a success psychology does generate success, and CCC's style in the seventies is more effective than that of many churches. Crusaders favor a schematic view of recent history just as they do of scriptural history: the fifties was the decade of apathy, the sixties the decade of the radicals, the seventies will be the decade for Christians on the campus. While percentage-wise Campus Crusade does not actually represent more than a minority proportion of most student bodies, they have made themselves highly visible. They like to say that, due in part to their work, Christ is now the most discussed person on the campus. It cannot be denied that Campus Crusade for Christ went into the seventies larger and more vigorous and more aggressive than ever, even as most major denominations were in a recessive phase.

CCC is mistrusted and resented by many people. Some students are put off by their manner. Churches and chaplains of major denominations often say their influence is divisive and sows mistrust of the church despite claims to the contrary, and claim they present an oversimplified Christianity which ignores, among other things, its social message. Many dislike the group's implied claim to present the "right" or "true" interpretation of Christ.

But the majority of students today are more likely to be mistrustful of the churches than of free lance organizations, despite the latter's funding by conservative evangelicals. They have been more successful in the early seventies than many ministers who went a long way to identify with the social and theological radicalism of the sixties. With an almost whimsical unpredictability, students suddenly tired of revolutionary chic in religion and turned to the nostalgic intensity, some of them, of the "Christers" who just told them to be saved and live a clean life like generations of plain Americans before them.

THE CHRISTIAN WORLD LIBERATION FRONT

Another independent campus group, however, has retained something of the aura of a fading social radicalism about its evangelicalism

—the Christian World Liberation Front in Berkeley. More than any other group, it has endeavored to carry the life style, terminology, and media of the radicals and "dopers" into Christianity.

One evening, I was returning fairly late at night from a visit at a home in Berkeley. As I passed Sather Gate of the University of California campus, a site famous in the sixties for many epic orations and confrontations in the heyday of protests, I noted a crowd gathered around a fiery speaker in beard and sandals, and a large banner reading CHRISTIAN WORLD LIBERATION FRONT. I stopped the car and went over. The speaker was indeed proclaiming the evangelical message in "hip" jargon.

Around him, in the cool of the summer evening, were two groups: a coterie of supporters, who responded with an enthusiastic "Right On!" to the strong points the speaker made and who took the lead in the frequent hymns; and a curious, amazed, and occasionally sarcastic audience of passersby. I talked for a while with a young lady in the audience who had been a professional worker for Campus Crusade and was now involved in CWLF work. In a southern accent which betokened a very different world from that of Telegraph Avenue, she related with some pride the work the movement had done to transform street people. She talked of Christian "crash pads" set up and of mighty battles between Christ and occultism she had seen.

The CWLF was founded by a former statistics professor at Penn State named Jack Sparks. He had worked with Campus Crusade, but in 1968 came to feel it was necessary to adopt new methods to reach the alienated youth of America. With the support of CCC, he came out to Berkeley with his wife and three other couples prepared to be God's people in the midst of the new culture. He let his hair and beard grow, and began dressing in levis and work shirts.

A split between CWLF and CCC was a natural result of the new departure in appearances. An independent organization was better suited to the mood of a radical milieu like that of Berkeley. Some of the conservative evangelical backers of Campus Crusade were disturbed by the image of the new effort. They could not identify real Christianity with long hair and expressions like "Right On!" But the whole point of Jack Sparks's experiment was to show the counter culture that Christianity was not "straight" culture, but a message beyond any culture and therefore adaptable to the style of any person, insofar, he would add, as it is not contrary to the Word of God. But dress and jargon are merely matters of translating the Bible into a foreign tongue. Indeed, in his "Letters to the Street Christians" the New Testament is translated, more or less word for word, into street people argot: "Dig it! God has really laid a heavy love on us! . . ."

The work of the CWLF has included not only street preaching, but also conducting "Bible raps" on campus, and publishing the Christian paper *Right On!* It has established several hostels and the Rising Son Ranch in the country, which serve as temporary homes for street people, runaways, and drug-takers. They are operated by mature Christian couples. Most of the young people who reside in them are not university students, but dropouts of one sort or another, often unfortunate people who have never had a real family life. As with Christian communes elsewhere, residents are not mature Christians (and should not be judged as such) but "street Christians"—"babes in Christ" who are making the transition from one life to another.

Typically, they will sleep late in the morning, study the Bible and talk about it for a few hours, then go out to "witness" by "rapping" with people on the street or passing out leaflets in the late afternoon and evening. After a few weeks or months, most will leave the hostel to put down roots in a more normal life style: becoming a student, getting a job, going back home. Some may relapse, some may just disappear.

The CWLF, presenting as it does a conservative spiritual message in radical garb, has understandably confused many people. It has been accused of being both left-wing and right-wing. Jack Sparks has with undoubted sincerity tried to avoid political overtones of any sort, but in these days of the radical politicization of American life they are hard to avoid.

The CWLF paper *Right On!* has published intelligent articles on current problems which do not, like some more simplistic movement literature, dismiss all social problems as subjective "hang-ups" which would be magically solved if everyone "accepted Christ." It generally claims the problems are real but that the Christian method is different, and its critiques are balanced rather than violently or partisanly ideological. In a sense, Jack Sparks concedes, the CWLF is "counter-revolutionary," but only because it does not put social revolution first.

On the other hand, it appears the public demonstrations of the CWLF has made are all against targets which would please political and religious conservatives: nude theatres, the Russian Center in San Francisco (over alleged persecutions of Christians in Czechoslovakia), the "radical" Glide Methodist Church, site of extreme experimental liturgies and homosexual "weddings."[21]

EVANGELICALISM, CAMPUS GROUPS, AND THE JESUS MOVEMENT

These large campus organizations, conveying the evangelical tradition independent of the churches, are (except for CWLF, which historically can be considered an offshoot of Campus Crusade) older than the

Jesus movement and have had a causative as well as a reactive relationship to it. In both respects, the relation is tangential; many movement people are indifferent to them, and extremists might consider them too "Establishment." By the same token, the basic message and flavor of the organizations has been little affected by the movement. But the rhetoric, and above all the climate of opinion in which they operate, definitely has. Because of their evangelicalism, they are reaping a harvest made possible in part by the peripheral contact with the movement, often only through the mass media, of countless young people of conventional background across the land. Along with some churches, they are supplying a transitional routinization of the spiritual process released in the movement. They obviously help direct it toward integration into the ongoing life of evangelical churches, and direct persons affected by it into the niche in American society which evangelicalism has always held. By and large they serve to reinforce in the movement, or in persons moving in or out of it, theological and social attitudes characteristic of traditional evangelicalism. But at the same time, because of their special closeness to young people and campus life, at least in matters of rhetoric and styles of music and symbol, if not in issues, they are doubtless somewhat more susceptible to changing mood than conventional churches, and so also provide a vehicle for the integration of the spirit of the movement into evangelical church life.

The sectarian communes and the campus organizations—especially Campus Crusade and the spirit of Explo '72—undoubtedly represent the two-pronged future of the movement. A minority will go the withdrawal route of the Children of God, and they and their children will be the Amish of the future. On the other side, the movement—not necessarily the original people, but the rhetoric, the music, the signs, and the basic themes—will become part of the heritage of ordinary evangelical Christianity, part of its warp and woof, indistinguishable from the rest except to the historian. But this will serve to revitalize evangelicalism in this generation. It can make it appealing once more to youth alienated from the things evangelicals have always been alienated from, even as it swallows up the Jesus people as a sociologically distinct movement. Many young people are far more "alienated" by elitist radical chic than by evangelical lifestyle values, given the appealing format in which the movement's forms of expression clothe them.

8

Other Alternatives

THE JESUS MOVEMENT has taken such a hold because it has provided an alternative community for a class which had already experienced alienation. These people sensed a difference between themselves and the norms of society. They were possessed by a new vision and a new kind of self-identity, which no one else, it seemed, understood. The drug experience, the new occultism, and radical politics gave them a feeling of being the firstborn of a new and mystic age. But the new age was crucified by the dark side of the psychedelic world and the apparent defeat of their political causes. The new age community had to find another identity in which crucifixion and dark powers had a place as real as that of "highs." For several reasons, as we have seen, the world view of evangelical Christianity was for many the most viable new identity.

However, there are variations on this pattern. Some subcommunities within the youth culture have had special requirements in the matter of finding a new religious identity. Some causes other than conservative evangelicalism have had success in supplying a new experience and identity. I will not speak here of the many non-Judaeo-Christian groups which are essentially associated with the sixties—Eastern religions, occultism, Neo-Paganism—though many of these continue to flourish in the seventies and also do a work of resocialization.

Among many Jewish young people a movement toward Orthodoxy has surprised many liberal parents and produced a coterie called by some "Moses freaks." In this connection I might allude once again to the remarkably high percentage of Jesus people of Jewish background, including some leaders such as the Alamos and the Bergs. As we have seen, Jewish converts—"completed Jews"—are especially prized and celebrated; this perhaps relates to the importance of the state of Israel in the apocalyptic prophecies and the role of the Kibbutzim model and Israeli dance in communes like the Children of God. The Jewish community in America has apparently produced a generation of young people seeking not assimilation, but fellowship, rituals, secrets, intensity of experience, identity models, and a way of understanding disappointment in secular values. Perhaps Judaism's own history as a partially alienated community within whatever society it dwelt makes the evangelical, pentecostal Christianity of the Jesus movement appealing to some Jews, as does, of course, the movement's appreciation of Israel and Jewishness.

Here, however, I will restrict myself to a few random Christian activities which are not in the ordinary evangelical tradition, but which seem to be meeting needs comparable to (though not identical with) those met by the Jesus movement.

THE METROPOLITAN COMMUNITY CHURCH

One example is the Metropolitan Community Church (2201 S. Union Avenue, Los Angeles, California 90007), a new evangelical denomination serving the homosexual (or, as they prefer, homophile) community. Clearly an idea whose time had come, the MCC has grown with remarkable speed.

Like alienated youth, homosexuals represent a distinct group within American society which experiences itself as a separated people, misunderstood and persecuted, and also a people with real problems of their own making or derivative of the way of life which nature and society have combined to impose upon them. Significantly, within both the youth and homosexual communities, it has recently been the evangelical tradition which has been most broadly successful in making the alienation experience meaningful as a prelude to redemptive experience.

A scattering of local churches of several denominations, and various cults, have long had whispered reputations as spiritual havens for homosexuals. But because their homosexual character was clandestine, they did not assume the role which the MCC has undertaken, to serve as the acknowledged church of the homophile community. It is far larger than these earlier groups, and it openly proclaims what it is. Thus, it brings homophiles as a community into the lineage of those, from the frontiersman to the modern "doper," who have heard the assurance that the evangelical God picks his people from what society would call "the bottom of the barrel" and makes them into a saved people—groups as well as individuals.

The MCC was founded in 1968 by the Rev. Troy Perry. He was licensed as a Baptist minister at age fifteen, but later switched to serve as a minister of the pentecostal Church of God of Prophecy. He was married at nineteen and had a family. But at twenty-three he accepted the fact that he was a homosexual; this led to the end of both the marriage and the ministry in the "ordinary" church. For several years he was in secular work. But a conviction that both facets of his life—his call to the ministry and his homosexuality—were valid led to the establishment of the Metropolitan Community Church.

His calling became clear to him, he says, when he bailed a fellow homosexual out of jail in Hollywood. "It's no use," the other sobbed, "No one cares for us homosexuals."

"God cares," Perry replied.

"No," was the answer, "not even God cares."

To meet the challenge of showing that God cares Perry began church meetings in a theatre and advertized them in a homosexual newspaper. By 1970 the church, growing with amazing speed, had established branches in several parts of Los Angeles and in a dozen or so of the large cities across the country where homophile communities are concentrated. A national federation was organized.

Rev. Perry, like all the leadership of the church, openly leads a homosexual life. A bustling, energetic, charismatic figure, he keeps a busy schedule of counseling, work for the homophile community in political and social circles, and church activities.[22] His theological stance remains fundamentalist and pentecostal, but it is not presented in a doctrinaire way, and people of a very wide spectrum of backgrounds, having little in common except their homosexuality, have been able to find a home in the MCC. Forty percent of the membership was baptized Roman Catholic.

Worship at MCC includes gospel hymns and vestments of a sort more commonly seen in Episcopalianism. The Bible is as authoritative as in any evangelical church, but Rev. Perry's interpretation of those passages which seem to condemn homosexuality are, needless to say, novel. Romans 1: 26–27 ("For this cause God gave them up unto vile affections: for even their women did change the natural use into that which is against nature; and likewise also the men, leaving the natural use of women, burned in their lust one toward another.") does not mean it is a sin to *be* a homosexual, but only to *change* deliberately from heterosexuality to homosexuality. Perry adds that he does not think Jesus was a homosexual, but says that he would have been called one in our society—he did not marry, went about with a group of men, and even let a man rest his head on his breast.

The congregation is about 70 percent male homosexuals, 15 percent lesbians, and 15 percent heterosexuals who enjoy the enthusiastic singing and spirited life of the church. Some 600 to 700 people attend Sunday morning services. The service begins with a "singspiration" led by an energetic director in a long white alb. Several hundred male voices raised together in song, supported by clapping and instruments, can be an overwhelming experience.

The call to worship, on the Sunday I attended, indicated the eclecticism of the church; it was from Kahlil Gibran's *The Prophet*. The service followed the usual Protestant format of hymn, pastoral prayer, Scripture, anthem, and sermon. The sermon was on the topic, "I Am a Somebody." It stressed the necessity of a sense of personal worth and dignity. It was relatively short and combined biblical exposition with knowing, and often hilarious, anecdotes of life in homophile society. Just as the Jesus movement churches make use of "hip" jargon, so Rev. Perry's announcements and preaching picked up frequent phrases from homosexual argot, and the congregation was clearly with him all the way through.

The long service continued with a reception of some twenty-five new members. Each was warmly introduced and greeted. Rev. Perry said something personal about the background and life of each person. The service then concluded with a ritualistic Holy Communion.

The members of this church do not rush off after service. They stay and stay, talking, smiling, giving each other friendly embraces, drinking countless cups of coffee.

Life together does not end on Sunday, either. The MCC has an impressive list of activities through the week. These include parties, a "couples club," dance classes, and a classical music group termed the "Society of David." Of a more religious nature are the Wednesday night prayer meeting and the "seminary classes" three nights a week for those studying to become ministers. Discussion groups deal with religious and homosexual problems. "Survivors Anonymous," a group of people having problems with suicidalism, and "Alcoholics Together," a group similar to Alcoholics Anonymous which attracts about 250 people weekly, indicate the special acuteness of these problems in the homophile community.

All of these activities have brought people together, and not just in large groups. Since its founding, the MCC has performed more than 150 homosexual and lesbian marriages, or in their term, "holy unions"—the word "marriage" is said to imply a family. The Episcopal service is used in these unions, except that "spouse" is substituted for "husband" and "wife."

One break with Christian tradition is certainly the MCC's requirement that couples live together for at least six months *before* the union is solemnized in church. But we are told that, just as with heterosexual marriage, when the partners meet and are married in church and have a common meaningful church affiliation, the success rate runs much higher than the average. Even if the MCC was only a place where potential homosexual couples met, it would be making a substantial contribution to the happiness of people whose principal meeting places otherwise are often bars. The Metropolitan Community Church is a radical experiment growing out of the original evangelical concern to "rescue the perishing" on the darkest streets who may seem forgotten even by God and make them into a household of God's chosen people.

CATHOLIC PENTECOSTALISM

Another movement related to the Jesus movement, though not exactly the same thing, is Catholic Pentecostalism. The "tongues" movement, after about a decade of activity in the nonpentecostal "mainline" Protestant denominations, became active in the Roman Catholic Church in 1967. Apparently it began among students at Duquesne University. Its originators had been influenced in part by Dave Wilkerson's book *The Cross and the Switchblade;* once again the pentecostal churches proved to be the ultimate source of far-reaching revival.

Once it began in the Catholic church pentecostalism spread with a wildfire vigor which almost excelled its Protestant counterparts. Besides Duquesne, the movement has important centers at Notre Dame and Loyola University in Los Angeles; Ann Arbor, Michigan, is the location of a national center which publishes a periodical (Catholic Charismatic Renewal Service Committee, Box 102, Main Street Station, Ann Arbor, Michigan 48107). National Catholic Pentecostal Conferences have been held annually. "Charismatic communities" have sprung up around centers of the movement; these are groups of people, some of whom may live together, others only attend "tongues" meetings, but all share deeply a life of concern, prayer for one another, and pentecostal enthusiasm. These groupings, which may cut across parish lines and even include many non-Catholics, represent an emergent form of Church life, and Catholic pentecostals believe they will be centers of renewal for the Church as a whole. The whole movement has reached 10,000 to 30,000 Catholics, including some fairly prominent priests and laymen.

Catholic Pentecostalism differs from that of the Protestant Pentecostal denominations in that it is generally quieter in its manifestations, less conservative in its theological and social attitudes, and more closely related to centers of intellectual life. In its context, of course, it has the flavor of being a radical new "breakthrough" discovery at the cutting edge of fearless experimentation, rather than a revival of an old practice erstwhile associated with rural cultural backwaters. (The Catholic cultural equivalent of what pentecostalism has traditionally been to Protestantism would be something like the cultus of Our Lady of Fatima.) This makes an indefinable but very perceptible difference in the type of persons attracted and in the atmosphere of Catholic pentecostalism.

A Catholic pentecostal meeting I attended in the student union of a Catholic university suggested this new-old tone. The room was crowded with people mostly sitting casually on the floor. Priests, nuns, and middle-aged couples were scattered among the students. I was told that about 30 percent of the several hundred people present were non-Catholics.

The meeting opened with hymns of the "gospel" type to guitar accompaniment. Then, people began rising spontaneously and speaking, not in "tongues" but giving testimony, expounding Scripture, offering an improvised prayer. The speeches were not, in the Quaker phrase, "cushioned with silence"; scarcely did one person end off speaking before another began. A lady told of being abandoned by her husband and needing the help of prayer in the difficult task of raising her children alone. A nun was concerned about the leadership in her house, but was thankful that her Superior had received the Spirit. A lady now a pillar in the pentecostal movement laughingly told of how she once thought she was a "good Catholic" just because she went to mass regularly and even had a "convert" to her credit; now she knew how much more there is and was. From time to time someone would suggest a hymn, and the singing would end in the low patter of many voices giving forth praise and "tongues."

I could not help but be struck by how determinedly Protestant the tone of this Catholic meeting was. None of the hymns, prayers, or scriptural interpretation had any distinctively Catholic concepts or vocabulary, as far as I could see. The Holy Spirit of the "charismatic" movement seems never to move a soul of whatever background to invoke Our Lady or the Sacred Heart, but only to utter such stock pentecostal phrases as "Jesus, we come to you just now" "Praise the Lord," "Yes, Jesus."

Next the group processed through the bright, cool autumn night to the university chapel for a late mass. Needless to say, it was almost as avant-garde liturgically as imaginable, though the thought occurred to me it might have been impressive to have capped the prayer meeting with a splendidly medieval or baroque liturgy, to effect a true *coincidentia oppositorum* of the two main poles of the Christian heritage. However, the mass instead continued the pentecostal effusion: we heard guitar hymns, laymen in lay clothes entered the sanctuary to play instruments and read Scripture, the congregation crowded around the free-standing altar for the consecration of the bread and wine. "Tongues" came forth freely all during the service, culminating in a strange and deeply moving wordless chant which many joined in with after the Communion.

Just as the pentecostal churches have sometimes been called a "third force" in Christianity as a whole, so Catholic pentecostalism fits into no mold. Within a Catholic context, it is neither "traditionalist" nor "progressive," neither liberal nor conservative. For this reason it is not the same thing as the Protestant Jesus movement. There is no element of cultural nostalgia about it. It looks back on nothing in the remembered Catholic past comparable to the Jesus people's revival of motifs of nineteenth century religion. Nor does it advocate a style of Roman Catholic orthodoxy comparable to the fundamentalism of the Jesus movement. While it may be far stronger on the deity of Christ, the reality of miracles, and the power and personality of the Holy Spirit than present-day liberal Catholic theologians, it is also ecumenical and open to varying styles of spirituality in a way which is scarcely "hard-line."

Though Catholic pentecostalism is not culturally or sociologically the same thing as the Protestant Jesus movement, it does have a similar overall function. It has enabled many alienated from a traditional form of Christianity to experience the power implicit in the teachings. Many of those in the new generation of Roman Catholics have been unable to apprehend reality in the traditional liturgy and devotional practices, rooted as they are in a remote European peasant culture. Nor have they been able to feel the intense institutional loyalty to the Church, fostered by life in immigrant ghettos in America, which their elders felt. Among many, in fact, too much tedium, paternalism, and parochial school education has induced a deeply felt negative reaction. A large number of them have simply stopped going to church. But for others, Catholic pentecostalism has provided a new way of experiencing the spiritual reality behind the Church's rituals and verbal symbols. Some have reported that, once they had the pentecostal experience, they wanted to start going to daily mass too.

The pentecostal experience has offered overtones of rebellion, which appeals to the new Catholic individualism, as well as a meaningful conservatism in that it reacts against the assumptions of bland, sceptical liberalism too. Because it adopts such an extremely Protestant American practice as "tongues," and because it rejects or ignores things which smack of Mediterranean-Catholic culture, Catholic Pentacostalism facilitates full integration into American life style patterns. Pentecostal priests often talk and gesture in the unpretentious folksy manner of a midwestern minister rather than like an old country *pater* or *curé*. It is an American acculturation movement in a generation of Catholics which felt alienated from its heritage by existing, for all practical purposes, in a cultural and life style environment quite different from that which nourished the heritage; and fond association with America's most distinctive and important spiritual creation offered revitalization.

THE MYTHOPOEIC SOCIETY

In October, 1967, an organization was established which presents still another alternative. It is the Mythopoeic Society (Box 24150, Los Angeles, California 90024), which was started in southern California, but at the time of this writing has about eighteen branches in various parts of the country. It is deovted to the study and discussion of works of fantasy, especially those of Charles Williams, C. S. Lewis, and J. R. R. Tolkien. These three British writers, called the "Oxford Christians," were well acquainted with each other. Each created in his fiction an elaborate secondary world in which the Christian world view was concretized. In the quasi-medieval realms of Lewis and Tolkien, worlds at once Christian and heroic—created by God, redeemed by sacrificial love, teeming with wonder, miracle, and tokens of providence—stand forth in splendid epic clarity.

In Lewis' Narnia cycle, a world of kingship and talking animals was made by Aslan, the noble lion who is its "Christ," a mysterious representative of the "Emperor over the Sea." Later, Aslan dies a cruel death at the hands of the White Witch who has enslaved Narnia; coming back to life Aslan breaks her power. In the end Narnia itself passes away after "the last battle" to be transcended by an even more splendid realm, a new Narnia of infinite exploration and infinite joy.

Tolkien's three volume masterpiece, *The Lord of the Rings,* constructs an even fuller subcreation than the seven lighter volumes of Lewis's *Chronicles of Narnia.* His "Middle-Earth," drawn from old

Celtic, Germanic, and biblical lore, is replete with elves, hobbits, wizards, trolls, and men. A doughty little hobbit named Frodo destroys a ring in which the power of the Dark Lord is concentrated in a scenario which parallels the work of Christ.

Both Lewis and Tolkien have created alternative worlds into which the reader can rediscover magic and transcendent meaning, or which can be laid against this world to reveal the Christian meaning of seemingly meaningless events and sacrifices. Charles Williams makes the point even more clearly; his subtle novels of sorcery, romantic love, and psychic experience take place in modern London. Titles include *The Greater Trumps* (about the Tarot cards), *The Place of the Lion, War in Heaven, Shadows of Ecstasy, Many Dimensions, Descent into Hell,* and *All Hallow's Eve* (two characters in it are spirits of the dead). All of these books bear moral and theological themes, even if the message is sometimes slightly unorthodox (or, better put, goes deeper than conventional orthodoxy).

The founder and president of the Mythopoeic Society, Glen GoodKnight (his real name) was close to a group of science fiction buffs as a teenager. Through them he learned about Lewis, Tolkien, and Williams. He says he was converted to evangelical Christianity by reading the last of the Narnia books, *The Last Battle.* GoodKnight, now an elementary school teacher who devotes virtually all his free time to the Mythopoeic Society, created it in order to share his enthusiasm with others.

The Society has a wide panorama of activities. Not only are there monthly discussions in each branch, but subgroups are devoted to the study of the languages used in Tolkien's Middle-Earth, the general study of myth, and original writing of similar stories. Mythopoeia (the word means "myth-formation") as a life style comes into evidence at the great picnics and parties held several times a year and at the annual Mythcon, a mythopoeic convention of several days duration. Members wear lavish and beautiful costumes from the worlds created by the three authors. These alternative realities are also represented in music, painting, and drama. The Society contains many people of no mean aesthetic talent; the productions are often quite impressive. Members in one area tend to live a closely intertwined social life, which may take lively and imaginative forms. Events such as an elaborately staged "kidnapping" of a member on his birthday, often with a mythopoeic theme in the costuming and scenario, are not unknown.

The Mythopoeic Society draws from about the same age group as the Jesus movement, and some of its members have been through identity crises as pronounced as those of any other young people. Some of its members are Christian, some are Jewish, some are still seekers. Some people, but not a large number, have been converted to Christianity through the Society. Although the majority are probably not strongly church related and enjoy the three authors more as fantasy than as theology, they have found power in literature derived from the world view of classical Christianity.

They have been able to see Christianity as liberating them for a life in which imagination, wonder, and fantasy are able to create (and move them in and out of) alternative worlds. It is a new Christianity dressed not in business suit nor levis, but in gorgeous medieval vesture. Yet it is not just a revitalized nineteenth century gothic romanticism either, though the Mythopoeic Society does have a craft-oriented subgroup called the "Neopre-Raphaelite Guild." Rather, it suggests another alternative for the alienated youth confronted with a society of rampant pluralism and instant awareness: Christianity as gateway into worlds of intentional fantasy. The work of these three writers suggests that it is only traditional Christianity, with its backdrop of cosmic drama and its central spectacle of heroic sacrifice, which is of sufficient mythic power to make such subcreation possible.

THE PROCESS

Alternative versions of Christianity offer another possibility. Not gruel-thin reductionistic versions, but imaginative structures as rich and dark as the great heresies of the past, in which God, Satan, and Jesus are as real as they were for St. Paul, but in which all have quite different relationships.

In the early days of Christianity, the Faith was presented in two different guises: the orthodox form which prevailed, in which Christ was a redeemer sent by the Old Testament God who worked in objective linear time; and the Gnostic, now considered heretical, which stressed salvation by having right esoteric *knowledge* of divine spheres and processes, of the origin of evil, and of the real nature of the soul. It in effect substituted mystical, intrasubjective processes and experiences for objective, historical ones; Christ was the envoy of the hidden God come to lead mankind back to him through right knowledge.

Today, tiny churches offer Gnostic and other esoteric variants of Christianity. Some sort of modern Gnosticism, perhaps inspired in part by the wealth of newly discovered ancient Gnostic texts scholars have made available recently, may be an important enthusiasm for some coming generation.

One of the more interesting of such groups, and one which in my opinion represents more than anything else a modern Gnostic sect, is

The Process Church of the Final Judgment (627 Ursulines, New Orleans, Louisiana 70116). One of its symbols is a cross over a three-horned goat's head. It was founded in England in 1963 by Robert de Grimston; a fundamental theme of his basic book, *Exit*, is the very Gnostic concept that "Only knowledge, deeply felt knowledge, can break the Cycle of Ignorance . . . As long as we are ignorant, we are locked in the Cycle of Ignorance; and the Cycle itself perpetuates ignorance . . . But there *is* a secret. There *is* a way to be free of it."[24]

The freeing knowledge starts with acceptance that there are three great gods: Jehovah, Lucifer, and Satan. They are battling in an everlasting "game" for the souls of men. Jehovah is God of strength, courage, discipline, and wrath. Lucifer is God of light, beauty, and immortality. Satan is God of separation and destruction. Lucifer and Satan must not be confused; Lucifer urges people to enjoy life and value success, but at the same time to be gentle and loving. Satan is he who drives men toward extremes, toward depravity and asceticism alike.

Christ is the unifier who aids believers in reconciling these divergent divine impulses. The Process is as apocalyptic as any Jesus group, believing the tribulation and the end of the world is near. They await it, in but not of the world. But they are Gnostic in that they closely relate the cosmic battle to intrapsychic conflicts. They view the impending destruction as the result of inner, psychological conflicts, and see it as a test through which they, who know its outcome, must pass. The outcome is that Christ must unite these three forces in himself. Even Christ and Satan are to be united, for Christ said "Love your enemies," and Satan is his enemy; therefore he loves and can redeem Satan. They say, bringing the drama back to one's own inner strife, "If that conflict can be resolved, so can yours."

Although the 500-odd members of The Process Church tend to come out of the same kind of background as Jesus people and follow strict and chaste ethical teachings, worship is more oriented toward self-realization. It includes ritual with candles, cups, and monkish vestments, telepathy, encounter sessions, incense, dialogue, and music with guitars and drums.

These four groups illustrate ways in which the Christian heritage so central to evangelicalism, or selected themes or variations of it, have provided integrating motifs for highly diverse communities. We must now return to the Jesus movement proper to put together some final thoughts about its impact and meaning.

9

The Movement and Christianity in the Twenty-First Century

OUTSIDE REACTIONS TO THE JESUS MOVEMENT tend to be intense and partisan. Because it is a rediscovery of a pattern deeply interwoven with American history and culture, it is not something we can look on dispassionately, as though a strange cult brought from over the sea. Nonetheless, the intensity, the emotion, the indifference to historical, scientific, or social critique which characterize evangelicalism seem strange to many moderns in this supposed era of cool and sophistication, as though they had come to us from another age by time capsule, or from another world. Yet often the coolest people do not react coolly to the Jesus movement. We know it *is* part of America, and the sharpest hatreds, like the most poignant loves, relate to home.

The Jesus movement strikes many educated people as the sheerest obscurantism, conceived in ignorance and perpetuated by mad zealots. Other people view it as the healthiest thing that has happened to American youth for a long time, a virtually miraculous return by lost sheep to sound morality and sanctified ways. Politicians wonder if it is making a generation more conservative in voting patterns. Parents may see it as good if it keeps young people off drugs, bad if it produces sons and daughters who are always talking a strange fanatic-sounding jargon, who always leave home to attend their conventicles, and who will not wash dishes unless the Spirit leads them to the task. Ministers and college chaplains rejoice if the movement leads serious, informed students to services and classes, but complain if it sends them away to other places where an allegedly purer gospel is taught.

In all of this what is most important to our understanding is to see the Jesus movement primarily as a religious movement. It is not just a psychological aberration or a social or political swerving. It has its source in the desire for ultimate transformation which is the ground of all religion. It asks religious questions and gives religious answers. Young people want something that is absolute, that they can believe in absolutely. They will respond to any person who is able to convince them—by clues that may not convince everyone—that he *really* knows, is *really* committed, and *cares.*

They sense professionalism and a "hypocritical" game in most churches, schools, and homes, and with the ruthlessness of youth reject what they sense to be role-playing. At the same time, they are deeply confused about the combined passion and role-playing of drugs, sex, and protest which rack their own culture. They are partly afraid of these things but do not know how to refuse them without a convincing reason. They need an equally strong counter, and they know that only in spiritual reality—ultimate transformation—can there be an equivalent power. It is transforming power, not rational answers, they want. The mystical and occultist alternatives produce experience, but (at least as they appear to the novice) a more ambiguous morality. Those in the Jesus movement have found, or rather have been given, transforming power and absoluteness through the old American evangelical and pentecostal lineages.

The movement is religious just because it is centered on ultimate transformation of the self and the cosmos, not on social reform or intellectual questioning. A new religious movement is likely to *appear* absolutist in its religious expression and conservative in relation to social, cultural, and intellectual values. Because it is or seems to its adherents to be the vehicle of a new spiritual experience, it will burst the bonds of conventional forms of piety—it is the short path way rather than the way of the official temple. It will sing new songs and form new groups. But because it is more intensely *religious,* that is, concerned with means of ultimate transformation, it will be basically indifferent to the surrounding culture, withdraw from it, or casually accept it as a matter of course, its gaze focused elsewhere. It will show much less concern for the problems of the surrounding culture than those established religious institutions which, because they are custodians of its normative values as well as dispensers of transformation, have a destiny intertwined with the culture's. The new group is living for an age that has not yet dawned. Moreover, the new movement may even seem reactionary insofar as it revitalizes past symbols and language. Even if its experience is newly discovered by the group, as far as it is religious it is recognized as being part of the highest religious experience of the tradition out of which it comes, and so will call up its symbols and concepts from across gulfs of time.

All throughout Christian history, like two brothers dwelling uneasily side by side, two styles of understanding Christianity and its relation to the surrounding culture have existed. One, which today is usually identified as liberal, emphasizes that Christianity must always accept the vocabulary, concepts, and established scientific and historical world views of the culture in which it dwells in order to be a viable custodian of the highest values of the culture, credible critic of it when necessary, and a bearer of the deep spiritual experience of affirming with Christ all that can be affirmed from the wisdom of all men. Its strength is that it is flexible within the ambience set by the culture in which it works; its weakness is that even though it may sometimes criticize, within the family as it were, it is finally bound by concept and vocabulary and world view to that culture, and runs a grave risk of dying with it, as did Greek paganism (however well liberalized and philosophized by men like Plutarch and Salustius) with the death of classical civilization.

The other brother is that Christian style we have termed the evangelical. It sees the Christian experience, and the lore that goes with it, as fundamentally *sui generis,* incommunicable in any vocabulary but its own. Thus it is basically alienated from culture—"Christ against culture," in H. Richard Niebuhr's phrase—and so evangelical Christianity and those who are alienated within the culture naturally feel a kinship for each other. Its weakness is that in the nature of things it will never live much more than a marginal intellectual, social, and aesthetic life; it is too inflexible *within* the culture, though it may try to advance those cultural and political values that at least give it living room. Its strength is that it is far less likely than liberalism to die *with* the culture.

Through Christian history these "brothers" have existed side by side. In the early days men like Justin Martyr and Clement of Alexandria represented the liberal kind of interpretation while men like the later Tertullian were evangelical. More than a millennium later, Renaissance humanists and Protestant reformers shared the dual heritage. Today, liberalism and evangelicalism split both Catholicism and Protestantism in America.

The Jesus movement is only a part of the perpetuation of the evangelical side. History, least of all the history of movements, never remains static. The only thing certain about the future of the Jesus movement is that it will not stay in its present fluid state. Already the trend is for the movement to get off the streets and into the hands of organized carrying organizations—evangelical churches, independent campus groups, and movement-born groups well on the way to becoming minor radical sects like the Children of God. But the evangelical wing of American Christianity will be strengthened and, hopefully, enriched through this process of feeding new blood into evangelical churches and creating a few new evangelical groups. In the process the liberal churches are made to appear spiritually dated and desiccated.

The importance of this strengthening, however, should not be over-emphasized. The results are not all in yet. As we have seen, the statistical significance of the Jesus movement is not great. Moreover, we can expect it to have a counter-productive effect perhaps equal to its positive effect over the long haul, as "backsliders" from the movement, by now well innoculated against any form of Christianity, increase in numbers, and outsiders (identifying the rhetoric of the movement with evangelicalism in general) never come near it.

We can wonder what will happen if all the Jesus people who expect the Second Coming within the next few years are disappointed. Sometimes such groups of radically disillusioned people are dangerous—I have heard concern that they might turn to something like fascism. I have even heard rumors that there are young people in the movement who say they are involved with it not because they really believe Christ is the answer and the Coming One, but because the movement is good training for them as they await the coming of *another* whom they are expecting! I don't think the numbers involved warrant serious concern, but these are trends it may be interesting to watch.

The greatest long-term impact of the movement may be in that it held a generation of young people of evangelical background to their churches. These are the sort of people who attended Explo '72. The fact that the movement has at least made evangelicalism seem in vogue and a live alternative in even the most sophisticated campus and entertainment-industry circles is doing much to counter the usual drift of better-educated youth from evangelical and pentecostal to middle-of-the-road or liberal churches. This helps insure that evangelicalism will continue to be a major force in American spirituality for the remainder of the century.

Thus the movement will probably end up as a cultural drift, providing a modicum of renewal to the evangelical churches as the liberal churches continue to falter. The movement is significant because it tells us there are those who feel that the strengths and weaknesses of evangelicalism and liberalism are being tested in a time of rapid cultural change and crisis, and that evangelicalism will win. Culture-affirming liberalism naturally functions best in a basically stable culture with a definite vocabulary and world view to which it can relate Christianity.

The evangelical, at least, feels times of crisis are first, when he comes into his own, for these are the times when those who made him feel alienated are themselves discredited and alienated as their world passes away; and second, when the integrity of his alternative reality, which depends on no world view but the Bible's, becomes apparent. If nothing else, evangelicalism is survival Christianity. Those who are attracted to it, in the Jesus movement and otherwise, sense a coming crisis of cultural transition, and in a real sense count on it to vindicate them. Sensing that liberalism is too bound to what is passing away, they are willing to bet on evangelicalism to provide an ark when the floods rise and the old is swept away.

The strains which increasingly will produce feelings like these in the decades to come are well portrayed by a book like Alvin Toffler's *Future Shock*.[25] It shows the anxiety and insecurity, capable of becoming almost pathological, induced by rapid change, social mobility, and phased obsolescence.

Against this, religion may be expected to throw up two not incompatible reactions: traditionalism and apocalypticism. Traditionalists will attempt to "hold the line" and preserve one area of human experience intact from change as a place of retreat and refreshment. In a day when much appears to be coming apart, religious man wants to create an eternally changeless alternative reality into which he can move. But at the same time apocalypticism increases. Times of rapid change give rise to voices wanting to trump the baffling mutations in the temporal order with absolute change predicated from the religious tradition. Both of these reactions, traditional and apocalyptic, coexist in evangelicalism and *a fortiori* in the Jesus movement.

A third possible reaction, mysticism, is not likely to take forms drawn from the evangelical heritage, since it is less congenial to it and has many nonevangelical venues.

Other strains in the coming decades which surely spell radical cultural changes will be economic and ecological. A book like *The Limits to Growth*[26] outlines the situation. This study, undertaken for the prestigious Club of Rome, postulates that the limits of possible growth in production and standard of living on this planet, given present and projected populations and natural resources, will be reached within the next hundred years. Given present trends, a crisis would be reached around the year 2020, and would be followed by a rapid decline in human population caused by starvation and pestilence.

Some critics have charged this book is overly pessimistic, and that the limits will not be reached for three or four more centuries. In any case, it appears that sooner or later mankind must learn the moral of *The Limits to Growth,* unless (this is presently highly unlikely) new planets are opened up for large-scale colonization. The moral is that mankind must change his economic and cultural values to a no-growth, steady state system, with attendant changes in spiritual outlook.

He must then accept a smaller world population and a simpler, chastened style of living in which he frugally recycles all material goods. He must find more satisfaction in cultural, recreational, and interpersonal goals, and less in increasing production and income. To make the steady state viable without unceasing conflict, undoubtedly the standard of living in the world would have to be approximately equalized, which would require no small adjustment on the part of the "advanced" nations, and a loss of expectations of "progress" in the underdeveloped "third" world.

Man will not change easily. The continuing crises, false starts, plagues, and international and internecine conflicts which will enflame the decades or centuries of transition will seem to some people signs of apocalyptic end. The ambivalence of Christianity in world history will become marked. On the one hand, Christianity's identification with the increasingly discredited Western values of historical growth and domination over nature will cloud its fate. But on the other hand, the role of Christianity, evidenced in evangelicalism and pentecostalism, in providing a spiritual home for the alienated and oppressed, and through them a judgment on society, may counterbalance the great tradition's historicism and domination, perhaps to the surprise of many.

Christianity has been the faith of European and American culture, but it is not strictly a culture religion like Hinduism in India. If the Jesus movement brings out the evangelical capacity of Christianity to be a counter culture religion as well, it will not be without meaning in a time of failing cultural values, even for those unable to accept its theology. It may be the first in a series of Christian movements offering spiritual shelter to those caught up in the years of trouble, and perhaps will contribute to the spiritual foundations of the ultimate steady state society.

If it is to do this, however, evangelicalism itself must be equal to the challenge. It will have to show itself truly independent of cultural idolatry, not idealizing a half-imagined traditional American culture, or trying to create a walled off evangelical subculture, or binding itself to the main culture through overemphasis on negativistic attacks on it. These things cannot survive—only transformed lives can. The special value of the transformed life is that it is free from dependence on time and place, on past, present, or future.

A peculiar heritage of the Judaeo-Christian tradition is the historical view of time unfolded in the Bible. At least in the last couple of centuries, the historical panorama of the Bible has been interpreted as indicating that, contrary to cyclical and mystical views of time, the stream of human time is a series of irreversible events which have modified our spiritual condition. The exodus from Egypt, the incarnation in Christ are moments in a linear time pattern stretching from creation to the last day. God is in control of it, working out man's destiny step by step. In the palmy days of Western expansion and industrial conquest, a sense of participation in this progression, of working with God's unfolding plan, gave indispensible spiritual undergirding to the effort.

But today time and history seem problems rather than opportunity. We tend to see the future not as an open vista of fair fields ready for the plow, but as an ominous dark void closing in on us. The past seems not a meaningful record of God's acts, signs of future graces, but a turgid chronicle of miseries or a place for romantic escapism. Thus the premise of the current mystical and consciousness expansion movements is that only in release from temporal conditionedness can there be blessedness. It is also the premise of "radical suburb" man taking life as a series of experiences rather than as a commitment to a task to be accomplished, for each experience is to be enjoyed out of time for its own sake.

But evangelicalism, with its biblical world essentially sealed off from ordinary history and directly accessible to all men, and its traditional representation of the alienated, is closer to a nonhistorical view of human experience than liberalism. The Jesus movement represents a discovery of this fact by young people on their quest for alternatives to historical time. In its experience-centeredness it delves into new potentialities for inner, timeless ecstasy, and it is said that Jesus provides this more vitally than any other stimulus. In its traditionalism, its affirming of old American hymns and attitudes, it resists "future shock" and offers safety valves from it. In its biblicism and rejection of most postbiblical history, at least in intention, it provides an alternative reality sealed off hermetically from the "terror of history." In its apocalyptic attitudes, above all, it postulates the defeat of history and at the same time offers an explanation for the current historical crisis. By all these means, the Jesus movement indicates a Christian alternative to that Christianity which is closely bound to linear, historical, progressive concepts of time.

The Jesus movement is not the only possible Christian alternative. Clearly the coming decades of trouble and transition will suggest a mostly negative view of man's historicity, and the ultimate steady state society will require a nonhistorical view of man's being-in-the-world, at least in comparison to our present understanding of what historical time implies as its spiritual ground. But there are other possible models for a nonhistorical Christianity than the evangelical. Such models could be found in Gnosticism, Christian mysticism of various sorts, and the "playful" Christianity of Harvey Cox's *The Feast of Fools.* The Middle Ages offer an image of a theocratic Christian society replete with timeless "cosmic religion" motifs—wayside shrines, holy wells, seasonal festivals. Medieval man valued mystical experience and held virtually a steady state, nonhistorical view of time between the incarnation and the Last Day. Doubtless possibilities taken from all these and other models will be tried.

But right now what has been tried most fervently in our society is the Jesus people's blend of evangelicalism, pentecostalism, and apocalypticism. That was to be expected, for it is the alternative to historical and cultural Christianity most accessible to the majority of Americans. It is a heralding sign that the era of liberal, cultural, and historical time Christianity is drawing to a close, and that the day of Christianities considered disreputable in its heyday—mystical, evangelical, pentecostal, apocalyptic—is dawning as we enter an era of the pangs of death and rebirth. It will not be the last such experiment, and it may not be the most successful. The age of extreme alienation may end as we realize we are all forced by the times to be alienated from much of the past and present. Certain things of science, humanism, and Eastern religions may also prove to have survival value, and may temper survival Christianity as they have cultural Christianity.

The religious culture of the steady state society will not be simply the reverse of the values of the centuries of expansion. Nor is it necessarily foretold by the religion of the late sixties counter culture. Some commentators, quick to accept the latter at its own absurdly exaggerated estimate of its worth, read it as the apocalypse, the end of all time as we know it, the new heaven and earth. Actually, the psychedelic-mystical counter culture was probably a movement on about the scale of the Spiritualist craze of the 1850s. That enthusiasm also produced literature, communes, art, and meetings which momentarily overshadowed the regular churches. Its most avid advocates proclaimed it as the beginning of a revolutionary new era in religion, culture, and politics. But it burnt itself out soon enough as a social phenomenon, though it left such varied legacies as the founding of serious psychical research and a feel for the spiritual power of American Indian culture (the "Shawnee Prophet," the Indian "spirit guides," the rediscovery of the shamanistic model), and the ultimate ends of these motifs are not yet in sight.

The Jesus movement shows that at least the exotic strands of the counter culture can be challenged on their own turf. The religion of the coming steady state society, then, will not necessarily be all I Ching, Tao, and yoga. In part, of course, the Jesus movement is a reaction against the very idea of a steady state society, insofar as that society implies a medieval or Tibetan world of hierarchy, static social conditions, and governance by an elite of technological or mystical adepts. The Jesus people are, after all, children of the Reformation. Just as "justification by faith" once meant "no priests," so "One Way" now means "no gurus." *Everybody* from the lowliest teeny-bopper on up is, in his simple moment of trust in Christ, equal before God. That they, like the Reformation churches, may have their own priest or guru equivalents is, for the moment, beside the point—the vision of society is egalitarian. While the chanters, meditators, and other followers of paths to spiritual realization under the guidance of masters still practice, they are not unchallenged in their deepest assumptions.

This is not an age in which the future can be seen, but an age of ferment, a Hellenistic or Renaissance age, in which many things are being tried out. Just as the Jesus movement retains more of the psychedelic culture than it allows for (and the Reformation more of medievalism), so the religious culture of the steady state society will, at least in America, retain more of the religion of America past and present than many who see apocalyptic change anticipate. All religious revolutions are as much changes of label as of paradigm. Medieval Christianity carried over much of pagan Mediterranean religion, and even Islam retained as its very symbol the crescent moon of the pre-Islamic cultus. Motifs of cosmic religion, such as seasonal festivals and sacred centers, seem to persist through all mutations of doctrine.

In the same way, certain aspects of American religion—organization on a parliamentary model, children's classes, auditorium-type buildings, rationalized lectures or worship centering on verbal communication, distinctive styles of publicity material—seem to emerge sooner or later in all American religion—Catholic, Protestant, Jewish, or exotic— though little of these were necessary in, say, Tibet or medieval Europe. Yet these things, as well as the doctrine and methods of spiritual praxis, are parts of the total experience of a religion and go into its formation of personalities. As things change, in some respects they will also stay the same.

The Jesus movement is a part of this process of new consciousness, adjustment, and reestablishment of continuity with an appropriate part of the American heritage by people who are, perhaps unconsciously, aware both of the need to create new forms of faith for new times, and of the final inability of religion ever to take a form, or a formlessness, wholly alien from the past and present of its cultural environment. They will see to it that evangelicalism has a part in whatever religious web is woven for America in the next generation or two. Beyond that, if the issue becomes more stringently one of survival versus culture, the Jesus movement, or rather a new evangelicalism, may or may not be sufficiently able to liberate itself from its own kind of cultural commitments. But the Jesus people have seen the signs of the times, and they have tried.

Notes

1. Undoubtedly one of the best to date is Ronald M. Enroth, Edward E. Erickson, Jr., and C. Breckinridge Peters, *The Jesus People: Old-Time Religion in the Age of Aquarius* (Grand Rapids, Michigan: William B. Eerdmans Publishing Company, 1972). It is a well-researched, documented, and lucid account of the movement across the nation. While sociological in orientation and method, *The Jesus People* is by no means coldly "value-free." The authors have favorites among the vivid personalities and groups prominent in the movement, but the engagement—related to the writers' own brand of evangelical commitment—is always responsible and adds interest to a lively investigation.

Two strongly sympathetic accounts are Edward E. Plowman, *The Underground Church/The Jesus Movement in America* (entitled *The Jesus Movement in America* in the second printing), (Elgin, Illinois: David C. Cook Publishing Company, 1971); and *Jesus People Come Alive,* ed. Walker L. Knight (Wheaton, Illinois: Tyndale House Publishers, 1971). Both books are fast paced, popular level histories and descriptions of the movement. Both give the reader valuable information on its activities; Knight also presents a manysided critique.

A more sober, yet also sympathetic, account from a churchman trying to come to terms with the movement is Roger C. Palms, *The Jesus Kids* (Valley Forge, Pennsylvania: Judson Press, 1971). Palms calls upon the churches to respond to the movement by providing adequate means for its expression within them.

Lowell D. Streiker, *The Jesus Trip* (Nashville: Abingdon Press, 1971) is negative in overall impact. The author describes his experiences among the Jesus people in an engrossing and sometimes humorous manner, while seeing it as the same fundamentalism he long before rejected.

Two articles in particular provide important critical perspectives. Robert Lynn Adams and Robert Jon Fox, "Mainlining Jesus: The New Trip," in *Society,* February, 1972, pp. 50–56, give the results of a sociological study of behavior and attitudes in a major movement-related church. They are chiefly concerned that the movement represents a turning away from the real problems of America, providing escapist solutions to the crises of adolescence.

Alan Watts, "The Jesus Freaks and Jesus," in *The New York Times,* March 29, 1972, p. 41M, offers a more philosophical criticism. This famous author of many books advocating spiritual attitudes drawn from Eastern mysticism harshly accuses the Jesus people of an arrogant, self-righteous Christianity worshipping an "imperial Jehovah" which is untrue to Jesus himself.

2. The word *apocalyptic* will be used frequently in this book. It refers to belief that the end of this world, the return of Christ (in Christian apocalyptic vision), and the inauguration of the paradisical kingdom on earth is imminent and will come suddenly. Usually apocalyptic indicates that things will get worse and worse until the world is undergoing its penultimate wars, plagues, and torments; into the midst of this, as a breakthrough from another order of being, the radical reversal of the Coming, Judgment, and Kingdom will appear. The writings of apocalypticists, such as, in the Bible, the Book of Daniel, Chapter 13 of the Gospel of Mark, and the Book of Revelation, use vivid and often bizarre imagery, and usually portray the violence, suddenness, and polarity of the end-times in stark terms, with man then experiencing the greatest imaginable extremes of despair, hope, and fulfillment.

3. Arthur Blessitt with Walter Wagner, *Turned on the Jesus* (New York: Hawthorn Books, Inc., 1971), p. 199.

4. Leon Festinger, Henry W. Riecken, and Stanley Schacter, *When Prophecy Fails: A Social and Psychological Study of a Modern Group that Predicted the Destruction of the World* (New York: Harper and Row, Publishers, 1964).

5. Gary Schwartz, *Sect Ideologies and Social Status* (Chicago and London: University of Chicago Press, 1970).

6. *Ibid.*, p. 212.

7. *Ibid.*, p. 212.

8. See Morton T. Kelsey, *Tongue Speaking: An Experiment in Spiritual Experience* (Garden City, New York: Doubleday and Company, Inc., 1968), for a history and evaluation of the movement.

9. Frederick J. Streng, *Understanding Religious Man* (Belmont, California: Dickenson Publishing Company, Inc., 1969), pp. 4–5. See also his introduction of *Ways of Being Religious: Readings for a New Approach to Religion,* eds. Frederick J. Streng, Charles L. Lloyd, Jr., and Jay T. Allen (Englewood Cliffs, N.J.: Prentice-Hall, Inc., 1973), pp. 6–11, where the definition is changed to "means toward ultimate transformation."

10. Joachim Wach, *Sociology of Religion* (Chicago: University of Chicago Press, 1944), pp. 17–34.

144 / Notes

11. Paul Ricoeur, *The Symbolism of Evil* (New York: Harper and Row, Publishers, 1967).

12. John B. Orr and F. Patrick Nichelson, *The Radical Suburb: Soundings in Changing American Character* (Philadelphia: Westminster Press, 1970).

13. For accounts of Christian coffeehouses, see John A. MacDonald, *House of Acts* (Carol Stream, Illinois: Creation House, 1970); and Don Williams, *Call to the Streets* (Minneapolis: Augsburg Publishing House, 1972).

14. For an account of the paper and its founder's life, see Duane Pederson, *Jesus People* (Pasadena, California: Compass Press, 1971.)

15. David Wilkerson, *The Cross and the Switchblade* (New York: Bernard Geis Associates, 1963). See also his *Jesus People Maturity Manual* (Glendale, California: Regal Books, 1971). Wilkerson has had much influence on the Jesus movement and the evangelical-pentecostal direction it has taken. His dramatic work with Brooklyn street gangs is described in *The Cross and the Switchblade,* which has sold over six million copies. Wilkerson's evangelical and drug rehabilitation organization, Teen Challenge, has some fifty centers.

16. Enroth, Ericson, and Peters, *The Jesus People,* pp. 54–65.

17. Hal Lindsey with C. C. Carlson, *The Late Great Planet Earth* (Grand Rapids, Michigan: Zondervan Publishing House, 1970).

18. Enroth, Ericson, and Peters, *The Jesus People,* pp. 94–98.

19. *Ibid.,* pp. 22–30.

20. Ed Stover, "'Moses' Fears Sect Pushes too Hard," *Seattle Post-Intelligencer,* Nov. 9, 1971, p. A6.

21. Enroth, Ericson, and Peters, *The Jesus People,* pp. 102–14.

22. Articles on Troy Perry and the MCC may be found in *Newsweek,* October 12, 1970, p. 107; *Time,* July 13, 1970, p. 46 and September 6, 1971, p. 39; *The New York Times,* February 15, 1970, p. 58.

23. See Kevin and Dorothy Ranaghan, *Catholic Pentecostals* (New York: Paulist Press, 1969); and *As the Spirit Leads Us* (New York: Paulist Press, 1971). See also John S. Phillipson, "Two Pentecostal Experiences," *America,* March 29, 1969, pp. 360–63; and Donald L. Gelpi, "Understanding Spirit Baptism," *America,* May 16, 1970, pp. 520–21, which includes a summary of the statement on Catholic Pentecostalism released by the American Catholic bishops Nov. 14, 1969.

24. Robert de Grimston, *Exit* (Letchworth, Hertfordshire, England: The Garden City Press Limited, n.d.), p. 29. An article on The Process Church (and on another group, The Way) appeared in *Time,* September 6, 1971, p. 54.

25. Alvin Toffler, *Future Shock* (New York: Random House, Inc., 1970).

26. Donella Meadows, *et. al., The Limits to Growth* (Washington: Potomac Associates, 1972).

Bibliography

Blessitt, Arthur, with Walter Wagner, *Turned on to Jesus.* New York: Hawthorn Books, Inc., 1971.

Daniel Yankelovich, Inc., *The Changing Values on Campus.* New York: Simon & Schuster, Inc., 1971.

Enroth, Ronald M., Edward E. Ericson, Jr., and C. Breckenridge Peters, *The Jesus People: Old-Time Religion in the Age of Aquarius.* Grand Rapids, Mich.: W. B. Eerdmans Publishing Co., 1972.

Festinger, Leon, Henry W. Riecken, and Stanley Schachter, *When Prophecy Fails: A Social and Psychological Study of a Modern Group That Predicted the Destruction of the World.* New York: Harper & Row, Publishers, 1964.

Graham, Billy, *The Jesus Generation.* Grand Rapids, Mich.: Zondervan Publishing House, 1971.

Jorstad, Erling, *That New-Time Religion: The Jesus Revival in America.* Minneapolis: Augsburg Publishing House, 1972.

Kelsey, Morton T., *Tongue-Speaking: An Experiment in Spiritual Experience.* Garden City, N. Y.: Doubleday & Company, Inc. 1968.

King, Pat, *The Jesus People Are Coming.* Chicago: Henry Regnery and Company, Logos Books, 1971.

Knight, Walker L., ed., *Jesus People Come Alive.* Wheaton, Ill.: Tyndale House Publishers, 1971.

LINDSEY, HAL, with C. C. CARLSON, *The Late Great Planet Earth*. Grand Rapids, Mich.: Zondervan Publishing House, 1970.

MACDONALD, JOHN A., *House of Acts*. Carol Stream, Ill.: Creation House, 1970.

MCFADDEN, MICHAEL, *The Jesus People*. New York: Harper & Row, Publishers, 1964.

MEADOWS, DONELLA H., et al., *The Limits to Growth*. Washington: Potomac Associates, 1972.

O'CONNOR, EDWARD D., *The Pentecostal Movement in the Catholic Church*. Notre Dame, Ind.: Ave Maria Press, 1971.

ORR, JOHN B., and F. PATRICK NICHELSON, *The Radical Suburb: Soundings in Changing American Character*. Philadelphia: Westminster Press, 1970.

PALMS, ROGER C., *The Jesus Kids*. Valley Forge, Pa.: Judson Press, 1971.

PEDERSON, DUANE, *Jesus People*. Pasadena, Ca.: Compass Press, 1971.

PLOWMAN, EDWARD E., *The Underground Church/The Jesus Movement in America*. Elgin, Ill.: David C. Cook Publishing Company, 1971.

RANAGHAN, KEVIN, and DOROTHY RANAGHAN, *As the Spirit Leads Us*. New York: Paulist Press, 1969.

———, *Catholic Pentecostals*. New York: Paulist Press, 1969.

RICOEUR, PAUL, *The Symbolism of Evil*. New York: Harper & Row, Publishers, 1967.

SCHWARTZ, GARY, *Sect Ideologies and Social Status*. Chicago and London: University of Chicago Press, 1970.

STREIKER, LOWELL D., *The Jesus Trip*. Nashville, Tenn.: Abingdon Press, 1971.

STRENG, FREDERICK J., *Understanding Religious Man*. Belmont, Ca.: Dickenson Publishing Company, Inc., 1969.

STRENG, FREDERICK J., CHARLES L. LLOYD, JR., and JAY T. ALLEN, eds., *Ways of Being Religious: Readings for a New Approach to Religion*. Englewood Cliffs, N.J.: Prentice-Hall, Inc., 1973.

SYNAN, VINSON, *The Holiness-Pentecostal Movement*. Grand Rapids, Mich.: W. B. Eerdmans Publishing Co., 1971.

TOFFLER, ALVIN, *Future Shock*. New York: Random House, Inc., 1970.

VACHON, BRIAN, *A Time to be Born*. Englewood Cliffs, N.J.: Prentice-Hall, Inc., 1972.

WACH, JOACHIM, *Sociology of Religion*. Chicago: University of Chicago Press, 1944.

WEISBERGER, BERNARD A., *They Gathered at the River*. Boston: Little, Brown, and Company, 1958.

WILKERSON, DAVID, *The Cross and the Switchblade*. New York: Bernard Geis Associates, 1963.

———, *Jesus People Maturity Manual*. Glendale, Ca.: Regal Books, 1971.

Index

"Acres of Diamonds," 25
Agapé, Seattle, 62
Alamo, Tony and Sue, 60–61, 66, 83–85, 122
Alcoholics Anonymous, 71, 124
Alexander, Charlie, 44
American Athletes in Action, 116
American Soul Clinic, 106
Amish, 25, 99
Apocalyptic. *See also* the Millennium; Prophecy; the Tribulation
  defined, 143*n*
  in Jesus Movement, 89–93
  in pop culture, 2, 13–15
  in time, 86–88
  present times as, 137
  The Process, 131
  prophecy, importance of state of Israel in, 122
  sects, 97–101
  Seventh-Day Adventists, 43, 93
  vision, 88–89
Apocalypticism, compared to traditionalism and mysticism, 136
Apocalypticists, defined, 92–96
Aquarian Age, 12
Arnold, Eberhard, 98
Assemblies of God church, 48
Atheists, 25

Beecher, Henry Ward, 42
Bennett, Rev. Dennis, 49, 62
Berg, Rev. David, 106–10, 122

Bethel Tabernacle, 93–95
Bible
  as visual expression of Jesus movement, 22
  class, 17, 59, 70, 79
  literally believed, 24, 70
  reading, 35
  time, 31–32
Blessitt, Arthur, 7, 62–63, 95–96
Bliss, P. P., 44
Boone, Pat, 64, 90
Bowen, Lance, 63
Bright, Bill, 114, 115
Bruderhof movement, 98
Buddhism, 29, 52. *See also* Zen

Calvary Chapel, 62, 73–76, 85, 99
Calvinism, 24, 36
Calvin, John, 41
Campus Crusade for Christ, 25, 62, 90, 112, 114–17, 120
Cash, Johnny, 64
Catacombs, The, 62
Catholic Charismatic Renewal Service Committee, 125
Catholicism, 24. *See also* Roman Catholic Church
Chanting, 17, 28, 140
Chapman, John (Johnny Appleseed), 42
Chicago Seven trial, Children of God at, 101
Chicago riots of 1968, 16
Children of God, 62, 122, 135
  described, 101–11

147

Christian Foundation, Los Angeles, 61, 66, 69
  described, 83–85
Christianity
  evangelical, 18
  liberal and evangelical, compared, 139
  historical view of time in, 137
  importance of speech in, 34
  in Roman world, 14, 16
  medieval, 140
  Semitic religion, 87
Christian Life Church, 70
Christian World Liberation Front, The, 117–19
Church attendance, 7
Church of God of Prophecy, 123
"Church Song, The," 17
Church, the, 78–82, 85
Civil rights movement, 4–5, 8, 10, 22
Communalism, 97–100
  Bruderhof movement, 98
  Children of God, 101–11
  Christian Foundation, 83–85
  Christian World Liberation Front, 119
  House of Emmanuel, 100–101
  Hutterian Brethren, 97
  in Jesus movement, 59, 98–101
  J. C. Light and Power Company, 90–93
  Koinonia Community, 98
  Mansion Messiah, 77–78
  Qumran, 97, 101
  Reba Place, 98
Cotton, Gene, 64
Cox, Harvey, 4, 139
Cozzens, James, 3
Cross and the Switchblade, The, 66, 125

Dance, in Jesus movement, 22, 28, 105
de Chardin, Teilhard, 87
Deists, 25
Dixon, Jeane, 91
"Drinking at the Fountain," 79
Drug conversions, 61, 62, 66–69, 70–71, 94, 95, 100, 104, 110–11, 118–19
Drug culture, 7, 8, 71, 112. *See also* Psychedelic culture
Drugs, Gallup Opinion Index 1969 report on, 7

Edwards, Jonathan, 39
Episcopal Church, 48, 49, 123–25
Evangelicalism, 24–50
  as short path, 27–30
  as source of U.S. religions' rhetoric and imagery, 27
  attitude toward American society, 36–37
  avoidances, 33
  beliefs, 31
  concept of time, 31–32
  confrontational psychology, 33
  defined, 24–25
  folk religion, 18
  frontier aspects, 39
  history, 38–44
  importance of music, 32

Evangelicalism *(cont'd)*
  Methodism, 39
  nonhistoric, biblical and apocalyptic, 138
  religion of initiation, 27
  religion of personal experience, 27
  similarities to psychedelic culture, 18–20
Evangelical rhetoric, 35
Evangelical teaching and practice, 30–35
Evangelist as shaman, 38–39
Explo '72, 116, 120, 135

Festiger, Leon, 21
Fiedler, Leslie, 19
Finney, Charles, 42
Flower Children, 16
"Four Spiritual Laws," quoted, 115
Full Gospel Businessmen's Association, 83
Future Shock, 136

Gibran, Kahlil, 124
Girard, Chuck, 64
Glossalalia, 45, 84. *See also* Speaking in tongues
Gnostic, defined, 130. *See also* Process Church of the Final Judgement, The
GoodKnight, Glen, 129
Gospel music, 64–65. *See also* Music
Gospel singing, 48
Graham, Billy, 20, 66, 116
Great News, New York, 62
Griggs, Russ, 109
Grin, Jacob, 62

Hentoff, Margot, 1
Hesse, Hermann, 15, 19
Hinduism in India, 137
His Place, 62–63
"Historicism," 88–89
History, and religion, 86–89
"Holiness," 39, 45–46, 49
Hollywood Free Paper, 61, 62, 70
Hollywood Presbyterian Church, 59
House of Emmanuel, 100–101
Hoyt, David, 109
Hutterian Brethren, 97, 99
Hymns, 25, 28, 32, 44

I Ching, 10, 67, 139
Initiatory experience
  drugs as producing, 9, 71
  evangelicalism as, 27, 30
  Indian shamanism as, 27
  in religious counter movements, 27–28
  short path to, 29
  tribal, 29
Inter-Varsity Christian Fellowship, 112, 113–14
Islam
  importance of speech, 34
  pagan motifs, 140
  Semitic religion, 87
  Sufis of, 27

J. C. Light and Power Company, 90–93
Jefferson, Thomas, 41
Jehovah, 131
Jesucentric rapture, 81
"Jesus Christ, Superstar," 64
Jesus movement
  alternative community, 121
  and evangelical campus groups, 119–20
  and psychedelic culture, 140
  apocalyptic theme, 58, 89–93
  as "cultural drift" with "carrying organizations," 57, 135
  as religious movement, 52–54, 133
  becoming sectarian, 71
  communes, 98–99
  cultural background, 54–57
  doctrine, 58
  egalitarian, 140
  evaluated, 133–41
  focusing on ecstatic experience, 99
  history, 59–71
  "One Way!" symbol, 63
  relation to drug culture, 71
  structure and forms of expression, 57–59
  worship, 58
Jesus People Army, 62, 109
Jesus People House, 17
Jesus rock, 22, 32, 73, 116
Jews, "completed," 58, 122. See also "Moses freaks"
"Jews for Jesus" movement, 58
Jordan, Rev. Fred, 106–9
Judaism, 29, 34, 36, 87, 122

Kabbala, 67
Kent State shootings of 1970, 16
Kentucky Faith, 3
Koinonia Community, 98
Krishna Consciousness, 20

Late Great Planet Earth, The, 19, 89–93
Leary, Timothy, 9, 11, 20
Lewis, C. S., 128
Limits to Growth, The, 136
Lindsey, Hal, 89–93
Living Room, The, 59
LSD, 66–69, 70–71, 106. See also Drug conversions, Psychedelic culture
  conversion during trip, 62
  experience as initiation, 9
  trip, described, 9–10
Lucifer, 131

McGready, Rev. James, 40
McPherson, Aimee Semple, 47
Mansion Messiah, 76–78
Maranatha, 62
Marijuana, 7, 68, 70
Maslow, Abraham, 11
Maui Occult Research Center, 22
Meditation, 8, 22, 25, 52, 54, 70, 72, 140
Meissner, Linda, 62, 109
Metamorphoses, 10

Methodist, 39, 41, 45, 78
Metropolitan Community Church, The, 122–25
Millennium, the, 93, 134
Moody, Dwight L., 20, 32, 43–44
"Moses freaks," 122
Music, 48, 59, 62, 64–65, 105. See also Gospel singing, Jesus rock, Hymns
  as part of service, 17, 74–75, 79–80, 94, 124
  important in evangelicalism, 32, 44
  recorded by Mansion Messiah, 99–100
  representing alternative realities, 129
Mystery cults of Mediterranean, 27–28
Mysticism, 13–14, 25
Mythopoeic Society, The, 128–30

National Holiness Alliance, 25, 45
Nee, Watchman, 78
Neo-Paganism, 121
New Thought, 25, 48
New York Bible Society, 62
Nichelson, F. Patrick, 55–56
Nichiren Shoshu, 20
Niebuhr, H. Richard, 134
Norman, Larry, 22, 64

Occultism, 13, 23, 25, 54, 61, 100, 118, 121
One Way slogan, 3, 55
"One Way!" symbol designed by Lance Bowen, 55, 63
Orr, John V., 55–56
Ozman, Agnes N., 46

Parham, Charles Fox, 46
Parks, Carl, 62
Pax americana, 4
Peak experience, 11, 86. See also Initiatory experience
Pederson, Duane, 61
Pentecostal Assemblies family of churches, 88
Pentecostalism, 31
  Bethel Tabernacle, 94–95
  Catholic, 125–28
  history, 44–49
Perry, Rev. Troy, 123
Politics, in youth culture, 13–14, 115
Pop culture, 1–16
Preaching, importance of in evangelicalism, 32
Process Church of the Final Judgement, The, 130–31
Prophecy, 75, 77, 88–89, 89–93. See also Apocalyptic
Proselytizing, 20–21
Protestantism, 20, 25, 29, 48
Protestant Reformation, 32, 140
Psychedelic culture
  and Jesus movement, 121, 140
  evaluated, 139
  qualities of, 11–14
  similarities to evangelism, 18–20
Psychedelic drugs, 5, 7. See also Drug conversions, Drug culture, Marijuana, LSD
Psychedelic experience, 22, 68

Quakers, 24, 79, 103, 126
Qumran community, 97, 101

"Radical suburb" man, 55–56, 138
Radical Suburb, The, 55–56
Read the Bible, slogan, 3
Reba Place, 98
Religion
   American, 24–25, 140
   and time, 72–73, 85, 86–88
   cosmic, 26, 140
   Eastern, 13, 23, 121
   monotheistic, 14
   of initiation, 27
   of personal experience, 27
   organized, survey of importance to students, 7
   pop culture, 25
   Semitic, 86–87
   Streng's definition, 53
Religious movement, 53
Revivals, 38
   Azusa Street in Los Angeles, 46
   Cane Ridge, 40
   Great Awakening of 1740s, 39
Ricoeur, Paul, 54
Riecken, Henry W., 21
Right On!, 61–62, 119
Rodeheaver, Homer, 44
Roman Catholic church, 29, 36, 49. *See also* Catholicism, Pentecostalism
Roman Catholics, in Metropolitan Community Church, 123
Runaways, 7, 60, 71, 94, 95, 119

Salt Company Coffee House, 59–60
Salt Company, The, 3, 60
San Francisco Oracle, quoted, 5–6
Sankey, Ira B., 44
Satan, 54, 80, 131
Schwartz, Gary, 47
Schachter, Stanley, 21
Scientology, 20
Seventh-Day Adventism, 43, 47, 80
Seymour, William J., 46
Shaman
   evangelist as, 38–39
   Indian, 24, 26–27, 139
Shamanism, 13
Short path, 27–30, 32
Smith, Gypsy, 44
Smith, Rev. Charles (Chuck), 73, 75
Snow, C. P., 3, 4
Sparks, Jack, 118
Speaking in tongues, 24, 31, 45–46, 48–49, 70, 71, 94–95, 125–27. *See also* Pentecostalism

Speech, importance of in Semitic religions, 34
Spiritualist, 25, 42, 115, 139
Steady-state society, 137–41
Steenis, Rev. Lyle, 94
Stevens, Breck, 94
Stranger in a Strange Land, 19
Streng, Frederick, 53
Sunday, Billy, 20, 44
Symbols of Jesus movement, 63–65

Tantrists of India, 27, 111
Taoists, Chinese, 14, 27, 28
Tarot cards, 67, 129
Teen Challenge, 62, 107
Testimony, importance of, 32, 80
The Church in Los Angeles, 78–82, 85
Tibetan Book of the Dead, 9, 11, 19
Time, and religion, 72–73, 85, 86–88
Toffler, Alvin, 136
Tolkien, J. R. R., 4, 19, 128
"Tongues." *See* Pentecostalism; Speaking in tongues
"Tribulation, the," 78, 87, 88–89, 91, 102, 111, 131
Truth, 62
Turned on to Jesus, 95–96
Turner, Rod, 64

UFO cult, 25
UFO group and experiences of "disconfirmation," 21
Urban society, as base of pop culture, 14–16,

Vietnam War, 8

Wach, Joachim, 53
Way Out, 62
Wesley, John, 39
When Prophecy Fails, 21
Whitefield, George, 39
Whole Earth Catalogue, 19
Wilkerson, Dave, 62
Williams, Charles, 128–29
Williams, Rev. Don, 59–60
Wise, Ted, 64
Women, role of and attitude toward, 80
World Christian Liberation Front, 61

Yippies, 16
Yoga, 8, 22, 26, 59, 139

Zen, 20, 21, 33, 52, 67